Public Management

Public Management: A Research Overview provides a structured survey of the state of the art of public management research. Looking at the enduring themes of bureaucracy, autonomy, markets and collaboration, each chapter introduces key foundational studies before reviewing contemporary research. Although originally intended to maximise efficiency, work on bureaucracy points to the problems of red tape, contested accountabilities, performance management, merit and public service motivation. Autonomy research asks whether reforms intended to free subservient agencies from red tape and political interference have delivered the goods. Are autonomous service managers more focused on the needs of citizen-consumers and more entrepreneurial in their appetite for innovation? Marketisation reforms take a further step away from bureaucratic forms of control by exposing public services to market forces of one form or another. Competitive contracting and privatisation put public services into real markets while quasi-markets and yardstick competition try to recreate these pressures without private ownership. Perhaps reacting to the fragmentation unleashed by unbundling and marketisation, collaboration promises to deliver improvement through voluntary processes of negotiation and exchange. Vertical forms of collaboration between different levels of government, or between governments and citizens, promise a better match between policies and problems. Lateral collaboration between agencies working at the same level are intended to tackle the so-called wicked issues that fall between jurisdictions or else to share services and unlock economies of scale. The book concludes by considering the new challenges facing public management from global warming to the rise of populism and affective polarisation.

Drawing on evidence from across the world, the book will speak to all those studying and practising public management.

Tom Entwistle is Professor of Public Policy and Management at Cardiff University, UK.

State of the Art in Business Research
Series Editor: Geoffrey Wood

Recent advances in theory, methods and applied knowledge (alongside structural changes in the global economic ecosystem) have presented researchers with challenges in seeking to stay abreast of their fields and navigate new scholarly terrains.

State of the Art in Business Research presents short-form books which provide an expert map to guide readers through new and rapidly evolving areas of research. Each title will provide an overview of the area, a guide to the key literature and theories and time-saving summaries of how theory interacts with practice.

As a collection, these books provide a library of theoretical and conceptual insights, and exposure to novel research tools and applied knowledge, that aid and facilitate in defining the state of the art, as a foundation stone for a new generation of research.

Language, Translation and Management Knowledge
A Research Overview
Susanne Tietze

Public Management
A Research Overview
Tom Entwistle

Philosophy and Management Studies
A Research Overview
Raza Mir and Michelle Greenwood

For more information about this series, please visit: www.routledge.com/State-of-the-Art-in-Business-Research/book-series/START

Public Management
A Research Overview

Tom Entwistle

Routledge
Taylor & Francis Group

LONDON AND NEW YORK

First published 2022
by Routledge
2 Park Square, Milton Park, Abingdon, Oxon OX14 4RN

and by Routledge
605 Third Avenue, New York, NY 10158

Routledge is an imprint of the Taylor & Francis Group, an informa business

British Library Cataloguing-in-Publication Data
A catalogue record for this book is available from the British Library

Library of Congress Cataloging-in-Publication Data
Names: Entwistle, Tom, 1966– author.
Title: Public management : a research overview / Tom Entwistle.
Description: Abingdon, Oxon ; New York, NY : Routledge, 2022. |
Series: State of the art in business research |
Includes bibliographical references and index.
Identifiers: LCCN 2021010126 (print) | LCCN 2021010127 (ebook) |
ISBN 9780367353742 (hardcover) | ISBN 9781032064031 (paperback) |
ISBN 9780429331046 (ebook)
Subjects: LCSH: Public administration–Research. | Bureaucracy–Research. |
Government accountability–Research. | Privatization–Research.
Classification: LCC JF1338.A2 E67 2022 (print) |
LCC JF1338.A2 (ebook) | DDC 351.072–dc23
LC record available at https://lccn.loc.gov/2021010126
LC ebook record available at https://lccn.loc.gov/2021010127

ISBN: 978-0-367-35374-2 (hbk)
ISBN: 978-1-032-06403-1 (pbk)
ISBN: 978-0-429-33104-6 (ebk)

Typeset in Times New Roman
by Newgen Publishing UK

Contents

1 Introduction

Public Management: A Research Overview provides a structured or selective survey of the state of the art of public management research. Selective because it is impossible to survey, even in the narrowest sense of the word, all of the work going on in the field. Characterised by Waldo (1968, p. 2) as 'a subject matter in search of a discipline', public management takes theories from the social sciences of politics, sociology, psychology and economics and applies them to the real-world problems of developing and delivering public policy. The curious mix of social science theory and the empirical detail of problems and policies from around the world gives the discipline both considerable scope and depth. Public management research is published in a variety of places beyond the journals specifically devoted to it. Choices have to be made. The choice made in this book is to review work under four main headings of bureaucracy, autonomy, marketisation and collaboration.

Bureaucracy provides a top-down or hierarchical way of delivering services in which the authoritative decisions made by politicians are implemented, in theory at least, 'with enlightenment, with equity, with speed, and without friction' (Wilson 1887, p. 198). Distilling ideas from ancient practices of hierarchical control, the classical management theorists (Weber 1978; Wilson 1887; Gulick 1936) identified a set of principles – rationality, formalism, accountability, merit and ethos – which provide the foundation stone for the theory and practice of public administration. Although subject to extensive criticism throughout the twentieth century (Merton 1936; Simon 1944), bureaucracy remains the yardstick against which all other forms of organisation are judged.

Alongside bureaucracy, public management has long recognised the benefits of granting organisations autonomy on the presumption that some functions will be better performed, or at least better respected, without the meddling of politicians or superior bureaucrats. While the contemporary enthusiasm for the autonomous form of organisation can be attributed to the new public management (Overman 2016), the idea can be tracked back to the first central banks of seventeenth century. Absolute autonomy is of course as unachievable as perfect bureaucracy (Hood 1976). In real terms then autonomy reforms promise in Berlin's (1969) terms a degree of *freedom from* something (like political interference or central government bureaucracy) with a view to creating the *freedom to* focus on something else (like a particular policy problem or the needs of the client). The autonomy idea is now promoted as a way of improving the management of frontline public service delivery organisations like hospitals and schools.

Marketisation too has a long lineage. Governments have always relied on privately owned organisations to deliver their policies (Wettenhall 2005). The notion that the market form of organisation should be purposively created in a bid to reproduce the 'vigorous virtues' of the private sector is though a relatively recent development (Letwin 1993). Marketisation – in the form of privatisation, contracting, purchaser provider splits and yardstick competition – is intended to recreate or simulate market forces which focus providers on the core business of improving services and reducing cost. Marketisation in one or other of its forms touches almost all of the functions provided or procured by the state.

Finally, governments appeal to the collaborative or partnership form of governance – with its emphasis on joint decision-making, the reciprocal exchange of resources and trust (Powell 1990) – to clear up the mess created by hierarchies, markets and autonomy. More formally expressed, organisational forms like bureaucracy, markets and autonomy all have the effect of focusing the organisation on a relatively narrowly defined core mission (answering to political principals in a bureaucracy or surviving in a market). This narrow focus can have unintended or dysfunctional effects on issues which cut across or fall between these jurisdictions. Typically then, collaborative forms of governance (whether labelled as partnerships or networks) are asked to address the cross-cutting or wicked issues best epitomised perhaps by global warming, which fall between the mandates of existing organisations.

This book provides an overview of key reference points and recent public management research in these four areas. Although inspired by the changing form of UK public management, the ideas at the heart of this book are not distinctive to any one country. Organisational forms (like bureaucracy, autonomy and so forth) are genuinely international in that they were coined and developed by practitioners and scholars working across the world. Reflecting the international flavour of the discipline, this book draws on work conducted in a variety of national settings on the presumption – which is not always well founded – that a study of marketisation in the US speaks to those trying to understand marketisation in the UK. The rest of this chapter defends the focus on these four themes before providing a preview of the remaining chapters.

The changing patterns of public management

The focus on bureaucracy, markets and collaboration has an established lineage. Hood (2000, p. 72) describes them as 'classic and recurring ideas in public management'. Based on Mary Douglas's (1982) cultural theory – albeit with different vocabulary – Hood (2000) looks at something like the bureaucratic, market and collaborative forms of organisation considered in this book. He does not include autonomy although Douglas (1982) does introduce the idea, albeit briefly.

Given that Douglas describes the autonomous form of organisation as one that befits the hermit or voluntary recluse who is 'off our map of social control' (Douglas 1982, p. 204), it is perhaps not surprising that her followers have found little use for this category. However, the idea of purposively granting an organisation the autonomy or freedom to determine its own operational or strategic priorities is an ancient and recurrent theme of public management. Alongside the creation of independent central banks, federal systems endow lower levels of government with the autonomy to develop distinctive solutions to the problems facing their area (Hooghe & Marks 2013). In rolling back the bureaucratic-professional structures of traditional public service delivery, governments increasingly use autonomy to unleash a new entrepreneurialism.

The focus on hierarchies, markets and networks fits with a number of other influential accounts of the changing shape of public management. From one perspective changes in public management are explained by the evolution of bureaucracy. Initially, at least, bureaucracy provided the backbone, even the beginning, of public administration as a discipline. From the outset, however, problems inherent in bureaucratic management prompted experimentation with alternative forms of organisation. Consistent with this focus this book provides a neo-bureaucratic or post-bureaucratic account of public management. Post-bureaucratic in the sense that there has been a significant movement away from bureaucracy to new forms of organisation based on autonomy, markets and collaboration. Research into these new forms of organisation might also be described as neo-bureaucratic because it consistently demonstrates that bureaucracy has not actually gone away. Many of the principles of bureaucratic organisation persist beneath the surface combined in hybrid form with elements of collaboration, competition and autonomy. Public management is neo-bureaucratic also in the sense that the principles of bureaucracy (in terms of formalisation, merit and so forth) have continued to evolve in ways that have taken them some distance from the original understanding of those ideas.

From another perspective, the focus of this book matches the changing descriptive labels much loved by public management researchers. It looks first at the traditional public administration of the mid-twentieth century with its heavy dependence on the bureaucratic model and constitutional convention. It moves then to the new public management of the 1980s with its emphasis on giving managers the freedom to manage, alongside performance management and outsourcing. Finally, this book moves onto new public governance's (Osborne 2006) (or even public value management's) obsession with collaboration and co-production. But rather than seeing these as distinct epochs in which public administration was replaced by public management (Lane 1994) this book sees these traditions as layered on top of each other in at times bewildering ways such that the elements of each are clearly discernible in any case study of real-world administration (Thelen 2003).

From another perspective again, the chapters in this book track continuities within the discipline which go right back to its very beginning. The epochal account of public management is persuasive only to the extent that it caricatures the instruments associated with different periods and refuses to recognise their presence before or after their theorised sequence (Du Gay 2003). Hierarchical forms of administration existed for hundreds of years before Weber coined the term bureaucracy, but autonomy too was there at the start. Although given particular prominence by the new public management, the importance of establishing distinct institutions with clearly delineated responsibilities emerged from the development of England's constitutional monarchy in the seventeenth century (North & Weingast 1989; Van Thiel & Yesilkagit 2011). Even more obviously, governments have always relied upon market mechanisms to provide goods and services. The early history of the private sector Bank of England in the seventeenth century provides case in point, but Wettenhall (2005) finds an entwinement of public and private sectors across a range of policy areas going back to the beginning of the state. While the boundaries of the state have been continuously renegotiated, the centrality of markets to public management cannot really be questioned. Finally, and admittedly largely informally, governments have always used mechanisms of partnership or trust to coordinate the different people and organisations involved in governance. Partnership is used more formally now and with extraordinary prominence as governments reassure us that they are working in partnership with almost every stakeholder imaginable. Other approaches could of course have been taken. UK focused public management textbooks cover management sub-disciplines like finance, human resource management, strategy, governance, regulation, stakeholder and performance management (Hughes 2018). Flynn and Asquer (2017) add an institutional focus to the mix by looking at central and local government, the NHS and the not-for-profit sector. Pollitt and Bouckaert's (2017) influential volume uses a comparative approach to track the public management reform agenda as it has played out across Europe, Australasia and North America. Comparative public administration acknowledges that differences in the social, economic and institutional environments of different countries lend themselves to distinctive policy styles (Richardson 2013). These factors and others besides mean that what works in one country might falter in another (Meier et al. 2017).

Other scholars focus on particular developments of broader significance for the field. Top of that list has to be work on the transformative effect of technology (Dunleavy et al. 2006; Pollitt 2012). Scholars working in this area describe developments in IT as ushering in a new era of public management by revolutionising service provision, data analysis and government-stakeholder communications. Others still highlight the importance of new research methods. In place of the traditional surveys and interviews, behavioural public administration emphasises the merits of building knowledge through carefully controlled experiments (James et al. 2017). Policy prescriptions arising from this research suggest that in place of the coercive instruments of hierarchy and markets, nudge promises to influence behaviour with subtle (and often very cheap) tweaks in the choice architecture (John 2018; Sunstein 2020; James et al. 2020).

Overview of the chapters

This book adopts a largely functional take on public management. Reflecting the practical focus of the discipline most of the literature either implicitly or explicitly adopts a performance-oriented perspective on public management. Does red tape damage performance? Does marketisation improve efficiency? Are formally autonomous organisations really free from central control? How can we get the best out of multi-organisational partnerships? However, not everyone working in the field, or on the edges of it, shares this functional perspective. Scholars writing from a more critical standpoint question whether the instruments of public management really are as straightforwardly functional as the literature assumes. Do politicians and managers use the rituals of bureaucratic accountability to protect and advance their reputations? Is marketisation better understood as a form of control than a source of efficiency savings? Are autonomous organisations more about symbolic reassurance than real independence? And do the new partnerships merely provide cover for the continuation of a neo-liberal policy of privatisation by other means? While this book cannot do justice to questions of this order, each chapter does at least point to some work of this type.

Following this introduction, the four main chapters of the book look at each of the main forms of organisation in turn. Chapter 2 starts with bureaucracy. Although ancient in its lineage, bureaucracy still provides the keystone for contemporary public management. Scholars continue to research the concepts of formalisation, accountability, instrumentalism, meritocracy and ethos first introduced by Weber and Wilson. Much of the time, however, researchers focus more on the dysfunctions rather than the functions of these things. In following the avenues of current research, this chapter surveys works on red tape, accountabilities and the problem of merit. Performance management and the idea of a public service ethos have been treated more favourably but even here critical literatures attest to significant challenges. While the central planks of Weber's bureaucracy persist, contemporary public management research describes them with considerably more ambivalence than was the case.

Chapter 3 turns to the mixed bag of autonomy-type reforms that promise to free functions from central management and control in return for the promise of improved performance. With a venerable lineage extending back to the creation of the first central banks, the autonomy idea has been applied in a variety of different ways. Currently one of its most prominent manifestations sees hospitals and schools given the autonomy to manage their own affairs. Whether used in central government (like banking) or local delivery (in the case of hospitals and schools), the performance improving potential of autonomous organisation depends on four lines of reasoning. First, autonomy promises to liberate those responsible for delivery from the problems of red tape and political interference. Second, it promises to empower decentralised professionals or managers to make decisions closer to the frontline of delivery. Third, it allows organisations to engage with, and respond directly to, the demands of citizen-consumers. Fourth and finally, it is claimed that autonomy can be used to foster a more entrepreneurial orientation and in turn a greater appetite for risk and innovation.

The twentieth century presumption that the state should take sole responsibility for the delivery of public services was exceptional. Before then and now, apparently once again, the state and market exist in a blurry entwinement. While markets are not new, the deliberate creation of market-like conditions – through various forms of marketisation – is a more recent development. Four forms of marketisation are considered in Chapter 4. First and foremost, governments advertise contracts to public, private or voluntary sector organisations on the presumption that the forces of competition will serve to maximise technical efficiency. Second governments have – particularly in the recent past – privatised whole functions in such a way as to offload the responsibility and risk of service delivery to private or public–private hybrids. Third, in circumstances not suited to contracting or privatisation, competition can be constructed through purchaser-provider splits in so-called quasi-markets. Finally, either alongside or in place of the above, yardstick competition can be used to encourage organisations to compete for rank in formal or informal league tables.

As with all the forms of organisation considered in this book, collaborative governance has a longer history than is usually acknowledged. Governments have always relied on high trust relationships of various sorts to access and then coordinate resources held both within and beyond the state (Macadam 1934). The formality and transparency of partnership working and its extension to ever wider and more demanding areas of public policy is though a relatively recent development. Chapter 5 looks at work on four fronts. First, it considers the varied forms of cooperative intergovernmental relations that have been developed to deal with the challenges of multi-level governance. Second, it looks at the more horizontal forms of network that have attempted to tackle the so-called wicked issues first identified in the late twentieth century. Work on shared services intended to garner economies of scale is then surveyed before looking at the relationship between public service providers and citizens at the heart of the fashionable notion of co-production.

Following a brief survey of the four main chapters of the book, the final chapter looks at the new challenges facing public management from global warming to the rise of populism and affective polarisation. Efforts to tackle these issues might be assisted somewhat by the development of new instruments associated with e-governance, nudge and policy mixes of hierarchy, markets and networks. Public management of the twenty-first century stands to be further helped by new research horizons opened up by experiments, new data and rapidly expanding opportunities for comparative research. This chapter concludes with the suggestion that the challenges facing public management in the twenty-first century require a continued focus on the big questions of how we make people and problems governable.

References

Berlin, I. (1969). *Four Essays on Liberty.* Oxford: Clarendon Press.

Douglas, M. (1982). *In the Active Voice.* London: Routledge.

Dunleavy, P., Margetts, H., Tinkler, J., & Bastow, S. (2006). *Digital Era Governance: IT Corporations, the State, and E-Government.* Oxford: Oxford University Press.

Du Gay, P. (2003). 'The tyranny of the epochal: Change, epochalism and organizational reform'. *Organization*, 10(4), 663–684.

Flynn, N., & Asquer, A. (2017). *Public Sector Management.* London: Sage.

Gulick, L. (1936). 'Notes on the theory of organisation'. Reprinted in Gulick, L. & Urwick, L. (Eds.), *Papers on the Science of Administration*, New York, NY: Taylor & Francis.

Hood, C. (1976). *The Limits of Administration.* London: John Wiley.

Hood, C. (2000). *The Art of the State: Culture, Rhetoric, and Public Management.* Oxford: Oxford University Press.

Hooghe, L. & Marks, G. (2013). 'Beyond federalism: Estimating and explaining the territorial structure of government'. *Publius*, 43(2), 179–204.

Hughes, O. E. (2018). *Public Management and Administration: An Introduction.* New York: Springer.

James, O., Jilke, S. R., & Van Ryzin, G. G. (Eds.). (2017). *Experiments in Public Management Research: Challenges and Contributions.* Cambridge: Cambridge University Press.

James, O., Olsen, A. L., Moynihan, D. P., & Van Ryzin, G. G. (2020). *Behavioral Public Performance: How People Make Sense of Government Metrics.* Cambridge: Cambridge University Press.

John, P. (2018). *How Far to Nudge? Assessing Behavioural Public Policy.* Cheltenham: Edward Elgar Publishing.

Lane, J. E. (1994). 'Will public management drive out public administration?'. *Asian Journal of Public Administration*, 16(2), 139–151.

Letwin, S. R. (1993). *The Anatomy of Thatcherism.* New Brunswick, NJ: Transaction Publishers.

Macadam, E. (1934). 'The relations between the statutory and voluntary social services'. *Public Administration*, 12(3), 305–313.

Meier, K. J., Rutherford, A., & Avellaneda, C. N. (Eds). (2017). *Comparative Public Management: Why National, Environmental, and Organizational Context Matters.* Washington, DC: Georgetown University Press.

Merton, R. K. (1936). 'The unanticipated consequences of purposive social action'. *American Sociological Review*, 1(6), 894–904.

North, D. C., & Weingast, B. R. (1989). 'Constitutions and commitment: The evolution of institutions governing public choice in 17th century England'. *Journal of Economic History*, 49, 803–832.

Osborne, S. P. (2006) 'The new public governance?'. *Public Management Review*, 8(3), 377–387.

Overman, S. (2016). 'Great expectations of public service delegation: A systematic review'. *Public Management Review*, 18(8), 1238–1262.

Pollitt, C. (2012). *New Perspectives on Public Services: Place and Technology*. Oxford: Oxford University Press.

Pollitt, C., & Bouckaert, G. (2017). *Public Management Reform: A Comparative Analysis-Into the Age of Austerity*. Oxford: Oxford University Press.

Powell, W. W. (1990). 'Neither market nor hierarchy'. *Research in Organizational Behavior*, 12, 295–336.

Richardson, J. (2013). *Policy Styles in Western Europe*. London: Routledge.

Simon, H. (1944). 'Decision making and administrative organizations'. *Public Administration Review*, 4(1), 16–30.

Sunstein, C. R. (2020). *Behavioral Science and Public Policy*. Cambridge: Cambridge University Press.

Thelen, K. (2003). 'How institutions evolve: Insights from comparative-historical analysis'. In Mahoney, J. & Rueschemeyer, D. (Eds.), *Comparative Historical Analysis in the Social Sciences*. Cambridge: Cambridge University Press, 208–240.

Van Thiel, S., & Yesilkagit, K. (2011). 'Good neighbours or distant friends? Trust between Dutch ministries and their executive agencies'. *Public Management Review*, 13(6), 783–802.

Waldo, R. (1968). 'The scope of the theory of public administration'. In Charlesworth, J. C. (Ed.), *The Theory and Practice of Public Administration*, Philadelphia, PA: American Society for Public Administration.

Weber, M. (1978). *Economy and Society: An Outline of Interpretive Sociology*. In Roth, G. & Wittich, C. (Eds.), Berkeley: University of California Press.

Wettenhall, R. (2005). 'The public-private interface: Surveying the history'. In Hodge, G. & Greve, C. (Eds.), *The Challenge of Public-Private Partnerships: Learning from International Experience*, Cheltenham: Edward Elgar, 22–43.

Wilson, W. (1887). 'The study of administration'. *Political Science Quarterly*, 2(2), 197–222.

2 Bureaucracy and public management

Public Administration's most important idea has somewhat ignoble roots. The case for a permanent, neutral administrative state bureaucracy recruited and promoted on the basis of merit was only adapted for democracy after centuries of monarchical service (Hood 2000). It is a history which takes in the Chinese Han dynasties (Hood 2000), England's Tudor revolution in government (Elton 1953) and Prussia's search for the most efficient and effective way of enforcing Frederick the Great's absolute will (Dorn 1931; Wilson 1887). Ideas emerging in Prussia were adopted by colonial powers in the nineteenth century as the deficiencies of a system oiled by nepotism became apparent (Greenaway 2004; Roberts 2020). Perhaps based on common theoretical foundations (Stillman 1973; Sager & Rosser 2009), the model of bureaucratic administration developed by Weber (1978) and Woodrow Wilson (1887) codified practices which had emerged in church, state and military administration centuries before (Höpfl 2006).

Bureaucracy provided the foundation for the discipline of public administration and it remains the 'go to' prescription for management failure. Inquiries into policy disasters almost always point to deficiencies of administration which can be corrected with more or better bureaucracy (Marinetto 2011; Dunleavy 1995). Scholars meanwhile continue to puzzle on what a good bureaucracy looks like. Contemporary debates follow the contours mapped out by Weber and Wilson in focusing on formal rules and processes, accountability, meritocracy, the ethos of the office and instrumental rationality.

First and foremost, Weber called for a rational system of administration based on formal rules. Such a system would, he famously claimed, be 'capable of attaining the highest degree of efficiency' (Weber 1978, p. 223). Formalisation has though fallen into disrepute. While the advocates of lean (Radnor et al. 2012) continue to research the efficiency benefits of formal systems, mainstream public management scholars spend more time researching the dysfunctions than functions of formalisation. Generating at best mixed results, decades of research into red tape might suggest, however, that Weber's system is not as inefficient as the stereotype of a creaking bureaucracy suggests.

Second, Weber and Wilson describe a principal-agent form of accountability. As Weber describes it, the 'organization of offices follows the principle of hierarchy that is each lower office is under the control and supervision of a higher one' (1978, p. 218). Both Wilson (1887) and Weber (1978) took the view that, organised in this way, the permanent apparatus if the state could serve either a monarchy or a democracy with 'equal facility' (Weber 1978, p. 221). Recent research questions whether the neutral competence envisaged by Weber and Wilson is achievable, at the same time as it points to a variety of different accountabilities to other principals and stakeholders.

Third, although not explicitly mentioned by Weber or Wilson, this chapter looks at performance management and target setting. Partly because they are associated (rightly or wrongly) with the rational and instrumental form of administration described by Weber (Broadbent & Laughlin 2009). And partly because both have assumed such a prominent position in the output focussed accountability systems of the NPM. While some researchers point to the successes of these performance management regimes, others claim that they are manipulated for reputational purposes.

Fourth, both Weber and Wilson envisaged the need for competitive recruitment and technical education. Wilson (1887, p. 216) explains that: 'A technically schooled civil service will presently have become indispensable'. Weber (1978, p. 220) called for candidates 'selected on the basis of technical qualifications ... tested by examination or guaranteed by diplomas'. Almost from the outset, however, researchers have questioned the definition and measurement of merit pointing to the way in which many selection procedures work to the advantage of privileged groups. Other research lends support to the claim that that politicised appointments have the merits or skills necessary to operate in political environments.

Fifth and finally, both Weber and Wilson describe a cadre of dedicated bureaucrats driven by an ethos of office. Both men describe the ethos as central to the neutral competence of the bureaucracy which would allow officials to serve their political masters irrespective of their political persuasion. Although largely ignored through much of the twentieth century, the idea that public servants might be motivated by a distinctive ethos emerged as important avenue of public management research in the 1990s. While contemporary research points to the many benefits of public service motivation (PSM), researchers also highlight some less desirable consequences at the same time as they ask important questions about the way in which the ethos or motivation idea has been defined and measured.

While the overarching themes of public administration have stayed the same, contemporary research increasingly looks at the flipside of the virtues described by Weber and Wilson. Instead of the efficiency of administrative processes scholars look at their antithesis in the form of so-called red tape. Rather than studying lines of accountability to politicians and their citizen principals, increasingly it is recognised that public servants juggle many different accountabilities in a variety of ways. Representations of performance, in particular, are managed and manipulated to show the organisation in its best light. Merit too has come under the microscope. In place of the relatively straightforward call for technical qualifications, scholars puzzle on the definition of bureaucratic competence and the benefits of representative bureaucracy. Interest in the ethos of office – so-called PSM – shows no sign of abating although it is increasingly recognised that alongside its benefits, PSM may have a dark side as well.

Red tape

Although the pioneers of bureaucracy envisaged a form of organisation capable of delivering the utmost efficiency, critics claimed that formalisation of rules and processes at the heart of bureaucracy breeds red tape (Merton 1936; Kaufman 1977; Buchanan 1975). Indeed, the challenge of defining and researching red tape became one of the 'most important' issues 'in public management research and practice' (Brewer & Walker 2010a, p. 233).

Bozeman (1993, p. 283) defines red tape as 'rules, regulations, and procedures that remain in force and entail a compliance burden for the organization but have no efficacy for the rules' functional object'. He explains that dysfunction may be home grown (internal red tape) or it may be imposed by the environment (external red tape), sometimes in robotic form (Bozeman & Youtie 2020). Red tape may be built in from the inception of new rules or else it may evolve over time (Bozeman 1993). The former is explained by deficiencies of decision-making whereas the latter implies a failure to adjust rules to changing context. Theorists further distinguish between internal red tape (as perceived by the employees of an organisation) and stakeholder red tape (as perceived by external stakeholders) (Brewer & Walker 2010a).

In practical terms, red tape could damage performance in a number of different ways. Unnecessary rules may waste staff time that could otherwise be better employed. Alternatively, rules may make it difficult to respond to the wishes of the principal or else to adapt to changes in the environment. Some rules may, however, prove counterproductive in that they might contradict or undermine the agency's mission. A motivation crowding effect may occur when excessive formalisation reduces autonomy and therefore motivation (Jacobsen & Jakobsen 2018). Finally, there are reasons to think that red tape will be associated with corruption. First as officials and their clients find it expedient to break the rules in a bid to deliver legitimate (or illegitimate) outcomes (Guriev 2004) and second in that red tape may empower (and potentially enrich) those entrusted with its application (Guriev 2004).

Although conceptually clear, the measurement of red tape presents challenges. Without singular or clear functional objectives (Rainey 1989), it is difficult to determine at what point the formalisation of public organisations tips into a disproportionate burden. The priority attached to different objectives inevitably varies through the organisation, such that perceptions of red tape will depend upon the position of the observer (whether they be managers, employees or stakeholders). Brewer and Walker (2010b) evidence this when they find that perceptions of red tape are inversely correlated organisational seniority. As Kaufman (1977, p. 1) pithily put it 'One Person's "red tape" may be another's treasured safeguard'.

Perhaps reflecting its subjective character, empirical confirmation of the damaging effects of red tape is thin on the ground (Brewer & Walker 2010a). One of the first studies (Buchanan 1975) found more of it in the private than the public sector. More recent work suggests that red tape has adverse effects on: organisational effectiveness (Pandey et al. 2007; Brewer & Walker 2010a), school performance (Jacobsen & Jakobsen 2018) and procedural satisfaction (Kaufmann & Tummers 2017). But a number of studies find little or only minimal effects. Blom et al.'s (2020, p. 18) meta-analysis points to a series of negative relationships (with leadership, innovation, goal clarity, communication and a set of individual markers of motivation) but red tape, they conclude, 'is not detrimental to organizational effectiveness and efficiency, and employee performance'. Brewer and Walker (2012, p. 110) conclude that 'red tape does indeed exert powerful, negative effects on performance, but these effects are not as consistent and uniform as the red tape myth suggests'. In a similar way, Jacobsen and Jakobsen (2018) find that teachers and school leaders perceive red tape differently, but it is the teacher perception that correlates negatively with objective measures of organisational performance. They also warn that: 'The widespread belief that perceived red tape is a substantial constraint on public sector performance is not supported' and that policy-makers should think twice before launching campaigns against it (Jacobsen & Jakobsen 2018, p. 32).

The dysfunctional effects of formalisation are also researched by operations theorists interested in re-engineering the quality and efficiency of public service delivery systems. Advocates of 'lean' argue that lessons from private sector manufacturing industry (and the Toyota Production System specially) can be used to hunt out the dysfunctional or wasteful formalism which plagues public sector organisations (Seddon & Caulkin 2007). Radnor et al. (2012, p. 365) explain that: 'Lean as a management practice' seeks to 'continuously improving processes by either increasing customer value or reducing non-value adding activities (muda), process variation (mura), and poor work conditions (muri)'.

Despite the enthusiasm of its disciples, empirical studies of the adoption of lean and systems thinking in health care have produced mixed results. Advocates point to reductions in waiting times, costs and infections (Radnor et al. 2012, p. 366) but critics like McCann et al. (2015, p. 1573) describe 'lean' as a 'fragile and feeble' initiative which has progressed through 'a prototypical fad life cycle, passing beyond ritual and into obscurity'. Confessing to the disappointing outcomes of applying the lean philosophy to the public sector, Radnor and Osborne (2013) argue that problems stem from a focus on 'internal departmental efficiency rather than external, service-user driven, value' (Radnor & Osborne 2013, p. 274). A reformed approach to lean needs to engage, according to Radnor and Osborne (2013, p. 278), with public services as services rather than as products and this means recognising their 'intangibility, simultaneous production and consumption, and co-production'.

While the service dominant critique of public management spear headed by Osborne et al. (2015) has merit, it is wrong to suggest that the value problem at the heart of public service delivery is easily solved. Radnor and Osborne (2013, pp. 279–282) argue that public organisations need new cultures which prioritise the experiences of the service user, but the problem of balancing the needs of the user against the interests of other stakeholders go to the heart of the dilemmas facing the public services. In our bid to root out waste and inefficiency (or red tape) we simply cannot assert the functional priority of one group of stakeholders over others.

The disappointing results of the hunt for red tape and waste in public service bureaucracies, although sometimes frustrating to researchers, is good news for the greater discipline. If, after decades of intensive inquiry, researchers have still failed to provide proof of concept, it might be about time to conclude that bureaucracy is not as inefficiency prone as its critics have suggested. Be careful who you say it to, but Weber might have been right after all.

Accountabilities

Alongside the focus on formalisation, public management scholars continue to focus on the way in which bureaucracies deliver accountability. Bovens (1998, p. 172) defines accountability as 'a social relationship in which an actor feels an obligation to explain and to justify his conduct to some significant other'. Bureaucracy promises a principal-agent form of accountability in which permanent bureaucratic agents are responsible to their oftentimes temporary political principals. Such a system had the merit according to Wilson (1887, p. 213) of directing 'public attention ... in each case of good or bad administration, to just the man deserving of praise or blame'.

The principal agent accountability envisaged by Wilson turns on the notion of neutral competence whereby bureaucrats deliver the smooth implementation of policies irrespective of their individual political sympathies. Kaufman (1956, p. 1060) describes it as 'the ability to do the work of government expertly, and to do it according to explicit, objective standards rather than to personal or party or other obligations and loyalties'. Neutral competence promised, as Kaufman (1956, p. 1060) goes on to explain, to take the politics out of administration or at the least to establish them as 'distinct and separable processes'. In such a way, a chain of accountability from bureaucrats to politicians and then in turn from politicians to the electorate would ensure – albeit in a rather convoluted manner – that the bureaucrats responsible for delivering public services are ultimately accountable to citizen-taxpayers.

Although one of the three core values to have shaped the history of American Public Administration (Kaufman 1956), 'neutral competence' conflated the separate ideas of administrative and political accountability (Hupe & Hill 2007). So while on the one hand the doctrine required bureaucrats to be guided by rules and rationality, it also promised the politicians responsiveness to their distinctive ideological agenda. While on occasion it might be possible to serve these two masters, it certainly is not going to be the case all the time. Tensions between the two forms of accountability emerged in the US, according to Rourke (1992), because both presidents and congress demanded a promise of responsiveness that a permanent bureaucracy would inevitably struggle to deliver. In such a way, the uneasy truce – between political responsiveness and administrative responsibility – promised by Weber and Wilson has been challenged by the politicisation of administrative appointments and the ever-increasing engagement of external think tanks, consultancies and lobby groups.

Neutral competence has come under attack from other quarters as well. The principal-agent form of accountability is challenged by a variety of stake-holders keen to exercise more direct forms of control. Alongside the public-administrative form of accountability, Hupe and Hill (2007) identify two other modes: professional and participatory. Professional accountability asks practitioners to adhere to standards set and policed by their peers in the collegiate structures of the professional bodies (Hupe & Hill 2007, p. 289). Participatory accountability is perhaps the most unsettling to traditional forms of bureaucracy in that it asks practitioners to answer directly to their clients and other stakeholders in a more collaborative form of engagement than representative democracy permits (Vigoda 2002).

Acknowledging the increasing marketisation of public service delivery, Thomann et al. (2018) add a market form to the expanding list of accountabilities. Public servants – increasingly working in the private and not for profit sectors – are accountable to the market when they try to deliver 'the values of maximal efficiency, profit, financial transparency, and growth' (Thomann et al. 2018, p. 302). Crucially these market forms of accountability are not the preserve of those working in the private sector. Thomann et al.'s (2018, p. 314) study does suggest, however, that private sector employees find it 'particularly difficult to reconcile the rules of the state with the incentives of the market'.

Alongside an increasing awareness of the multiple accountabilities juggled by public servants, scholars are focussing increasingly on *how* individuals and organisations fulfil their accountability roles. In exploring these processes from a 'reputational perspective', Busuioc and Lodge (2016) suggest that both account giver and account holder might be more concerned by the management of their reputations than fulfilling the needs of a formal accountability process. As they explain:

> From a reputational perspective, accountability is not about reducing "information asymmetry," moral duties, containing agency losses, or ensuring that agents stay committed to the original terms of their mandate. Instead, accountability—in terms of holding and giving— is about advancing one's own reputation vis-à-vis different audiences.
> (Busuioc & Lodge 2017, p. 92)

Seeing accountability processes from a reputational perspective makes sense of the symbolic theatre of accountability in which both account holders and account givers are judged on their performance in high-profile scrutiny events. But it also explains a tendency to simply go through the motions of routine audit and regulation in the cheapest way possible because the detail of compliance are unlikely to be of reputational significance. Finally, it suggests that on occasion, both account givers and account holders may want to distance themselves from their formal accountability relationships and focus on building their reputations with other audiences (Busuioc & Lodge 2017).

Recent work on the complex interaction of accountabilities suggests that Wilson's confidence in the smooth working of bureaucratic processes of control may have been misplaced. Partly this is because, as Weber suggested, the monopoly of knowledge enjoyed by the bureaucracy (Weber 1978) makes it difficult to control but it is also because the very idea of accountability itself is open to such a wide variety of different interpretations. With so many different accountabilities it is far from clear as Wilson (1887, p. 213) put it who or what 'is deserving of praise or blame'.

Performance management and target setting

Unlike the other themes considered in this chapter, performance management and target setting do not get much of a mention in the work of Weber and Wilson. The management of performance information is though entirely consistent with, and in a sense the logical conclusion of, the rational and instrumental form of administration described by Weber (Broadbent & Laughlin 2009). Although not a central feature of Weber's or Wilson's work, some of the other classical management theorists, not least Taylor, gave performance management more attention ensuring it a prominent place in the private sector management techniques of the twentieth century (Hood 2012).

Aside from a period of economic planning in the Second World War (and a more extended period in the former Soviet Union) performance management did not have a central position in public service management until the late twentieth century. It was the peculiar rag bag of themes of the NPM – and the encouragement to learn lessons from private sector management – which gave performance management its current prominence (Hood 1991). Without much in the way of theoretical underpinning, Behn (2003) claims that performance management can advance eight managerial purposes (evaluation, control, budgeting, motivation, promotion, celebration, learning and improvement).

Focussing on the last of these, Boyne and Chen (2007, p. 455) explain that organisational performance is 'likely to be improved by setting clear targets, developing detailed plans, and closely monitoring progress'. In a study of a target and reward programme operating in England's education departments, Boyne and Chen (2007) do indeed find that reward targets lead to performance improvement. Their findings are confirmed by Gerrish's (2016) meta-analysis of 49 studies of performance management. Gerrish (2016, p. 62) reports that 'performance management systems tend to have a small but positive average impact on performance in public organizations'.

Observing, however, that the improvement effect of performance management is really quite modest, Gerrish (2016, p. 62) concludes that it is the good management of performance regimes that really makes a difference. With a mean effect that 'is two or three times as large', best practice performance management promises significantly greater benefits than just bottomdoing it in a perfunctory manner. Gerrish (2016) includes in his measure of best practice: up target setting, bench marking and output measurement. Perhaps not surprisingly it seems that it is the manner of performance management rather than performance management per se that makes a difference.

In puzzling on why performance management may or may not work, Dubnick (2005) makes the important point that it is the 'social mechanisms' associated with performance management regimes that determine the link between accountability and performance. While some of those mechanisms may work in a functional way, a number of studies point to the dysfunctional behaviours associated with performance management. Reviewing, amongst other things the Soviet Union's experience with taut planning, Hood (2012) points to a number of the dysfunctional mechanisms which frustrate attempts to manage performance. Targets in particular may be associated with a series of gaming behaviours (ratchet effects, threshold effects and output distortions) intended to advantage the individual or organisation in their efforts to play the system (Bevan & Hood 2006).

Following Mary Douglas's (1982) grid group theory, Hood (2012) argues that the functional or dysfunctional effect of performance management regimes depends upon the culture of the organisation that they are applied to. Target setting fits most comfortably with a hierarchical (or bureaucratic) culture in which public servants accept the legitimacy of top-down forms of control. Ranking or league table-type systems (intended to cultivate tournaments or benchmarking) work best with competitive or individualist cultures which give public servants the autonomy to outwit the competition. Intelligence-type systems (where performance information is intended to inform the decision-making of producers and consumers) align with the empowering effects of egalitarian forms of organisation. Finally, Hood (2012, p. S90) warns that in a fatalist culture:

> it will be hard to persuade those affected that performance numbers really mean anything, that effort or talent put into performance improvement will be reliably rewarded, or that the management regime will not be undermined by chance and happenstance.

While it might be assumed that the dysfunctional effects of performance management regimes are restricted to those operating at the frontline of public service delivery, Hood and Piotrowska (2020) use UK public expenditure data to illustrate the way in which central government itself uses 'creative categorization' to game public accounts. Rather than providing an objective way of holding public servants to account, performance management systems seem to be used performatively by those both at the top and bottom of government in a bid to manage their reputations. While the evidence suggests that performance management improves performance, in circumstances where gaming is as prominent as Hood (2012) suggests, it is not clear what performance really means.

Meritocracy

The founders of bureaucracy treated merit in relatively straightforward terms. For them problems of maladministration, retention and corruption in pre-bureaucratic administration stemmed from a lack of regard to merit in recruitment. Appointments were made because of who, rather than what, the appointee knew (Greenaway 2004). Requiring that appointees should know something – anything – and that this should be demonstrated through qualifications and competitive examinations was a radical departure from existing practice.

There is some evidence to support this relatively straightforward approach to merit. Rauch and Evans (2000, p. 658) find that 'the level of meritocratic recruitment seemed to reduce the level of corruption'. Dahlström et al. (2012, p. 664) supports this finding, suggesting that employment 'based on skills' and not depending on 'political connections' serves to deter corruption. As Young (1994) powerfully illustrates, however, merit is both a slippery and at times dangerous term. It was used by the founding fathers of bureaucracy as code for the recruitment of a different sort of public servant. Pre-bureaucratic public servants had their merits – in terms of loyalty, trust and personal knowledge – but these were not the kind of merits valued by the advocates of bureaucracy. Although Weber (1978) and Wilson (1887) are not very specific about their preferred form of merit, they are clear that decision-making should be based on the application of rational principles. The advent of bureaucracy did not herald the arrival of merit-based appointment, but rather a change in the definition of merit. As Kearny and Hays (1985, p. 62) persuasively argue, 'politics has always driven the selection process in government'.

The understanding of merit and the way in which it should be assessed has changed over time. Building on Groeneveld and Van de Walle (2010), it is possible to identify a series of distinct logics running through debates about bureaucratic merit. While, as Groeneveld and Van de Walle (2010) suggest, these debates have evolved over time, new forms of merit seem to be layered above, rather than replace, pre-existing forms (Thelen 2003). In such a way, the pre-bureaucratic reliance on patronage has not entirely disappeared. UK MPs, for example, still defend the merits of appointing their relations to their personal staffs. While the evolution of merit in sequential terms is as Groeneveld and Van de Walle (2010) suggest an important part of the story, it may be more helpful to think of evolution occurring in parallel as different forms of merit jostle alongside each other.

The first and most significant challenge to the merits of patronage came from reforms which in the UK at least focused recruitment on broad measures of education. While the expansion of the federal bureaucracy in the US after the Pendleton Act of 1883 was built on 'specialized expertise' (Kearny & Hays 1985; Meier & Hawes 2009), bureaucratic recruitment in the UK emphasised general measures of educational performance. These early merit systems had a tendency to reserve bureaucratic service to a relatively wealthy elite who could afford the fees for school and university education. Aside from coming from the right sort of stock, UK selection processes provided for a bureaucracy staffed by 'gifted generalists' who without any specific knowledge of any one discipline had the merit of bureaucratic neutrality. A tendency reinforced in government by human resource practices which moved officials between departments with surprising frequency.

Critics argued that although the gifted generalists demonstrated a remarkable facility in turning their hands to new topics, their grasp of technical detail was not as secure as it might be. As policy agendas became increasingly complex, calls for merit to be defined not in terms of educational aptitude but specific knowledge in a range of technical areas became harder to resist (Fry 1969). But again behind the veil of merit, the technocratic argument was as much about the sort of people who should be in charge as it was about their training or expertise. The case for a more technocratic bureaucracy oftentimes came from the cadre of publicly educated professionals with careers and expertise developed in service delivery rather than policymaking.

Alongside the emphasis on technical expertise, the 'equality of opportunity phase' described by Groeneveld and Van de Walle (2010) saw critics call for a more representative bureaucracy which better reflected the demographic composition of the population it served. Appointees would still have to win their job on merit, but greater efforts were made to ensure that recruitment processes afforded equality of opportunity to groups effectively excluded by the earlier definition of merit. Crucially, however, while critics wanted recruitment processes which were blind to differences of sex, class and ethnicity, neutral decision-making was to be unsullied by these group identities. Representation was intended to be passive in the sense that the decision-makers reflected population diversity, but decision-making would continue to be marked by impartiality and the active representation of the interests of a particular groups avoided at all costs (Lim 2006). A more representative bureaucracy would have an 'enhanced legitimacy' which in turn 'seems to influence the extent to which clients and citizens cooperate and comply with government' (Riccucci & Van Ryzin 2017, p. 27; Meier & Nicholson-Crotty 2006).

Recognising that the processes of bureaucracy cannot be implemented with objective neutrality (Meier & Hawes 2009), and that the distinction between passive and active representation may not be as clear cut as Mosher had suggested (Mosher 1968; Lim 2006), the third diversity stage suggests the need for something more than race and gender blind recruitment processes. If diversity is desirable, then there is a good case for affirmative action to seek it out. Furthermore, in marked contrast to the equal opportunity phase, commentators increasingly call for the newly diverse bureaucracy to have regard for their constituencies in day-to-day decision-making. Neutral decision-making is replaced by active representation in which officials bring the insights of their identity into decision-making process as they seek to redesign policy and service delivery processes around the needs of marginalised sections of the community. While some critics have resisted the departure from neutral or impartial administration, a number of scholars (Lim 2006; Park & Liang 2020) find some evidence that the active representation of the historically marginalised makes for better performance for all.

Alongside calls for merit to be defined in terms of technical qualifications and more active representation, older forms of merit have not entirely disappeared. Indeed, politicised patronage appointments seem to be enjoying something of a revival. Peters and Pierre (2004,

p. 2) define politicisation as 'the substitution of political criteria for merit-based criteria in the selection, retention, promotion, rewards, and disciplining of members of the public service'. Research into the consequences of that politicisation point to more nuanced conclusions than the doctrine of neutral competence might suggest. Drawing on the very different approaches of Sweden and Denmark, Christiansen et al. (2016) suggest that the appointment of political advisers can serve to protect permanent civil servants from day to day or functional politicisation, freeing them to adopt a more independent and critical role in the provision of policy advice. In countries with few political advisers, by contrast, permanent officials inevitably become more embroiled in party political matters and struggle as a result to speak truth to power. Based on the way in which a sample of senior civil servants respond to a series of vignettes, Ebinger et al. (2019) also question the presumption that politicisation inevitably leads to increased responsiveness to political masters and decreased responsibility to the public.

While political appointments to the bureaucracy may in part be driven by pre-bureaucratic nepotism, they are at least to a significant degree explained by a search for a skillset under-represented amongst traditional bureaucrats. From this perspective merit can be defined in terms of political craft expressed in the form of sensitivity, strategy and communication skills (Bach & Veit 2018). Unpacking the type of trust and skill lying behind political appointments, Panizza et al. (2019) identify four distinct patronage roles apparent across different political systems: party professionals, programme technocrats, apparatchiks and political agents. Based on a survey of party patronage in 22 countries, Kopecký et al. (2016, p. 428) argue that it is inappropriate to assume 'a simple dichotomy between political and professional appointments, as politicians appear to be interested in both professional competence and political loyalty'. Control of 'policy-making and implementation is' they conclude 'the most common motivation for making political appointments' (Kopecký et al. 2016, p. 428).

Weber and Wilson proposed a system of merit-based appointment because they saw it as key to the neutral administration of the law. Their ideas are now questioned by advocates of politicisation and active representation who argue that neutrality does not work. Aside from Weber and Wilson's 'hypothetical bureaucracy', Meier (2019, p. 42) explains that in the real world, bureaucracy represents and entrenches the interests of the haves over the have-nots. 'Representative bureaucracy', he explains, 'can be seen as an effort to lessen the inherent biases of the bureaucracy rather than infuse biases where none existed before' (Meier 2019, p. 43).

Public service motivation

Both Weber and Wilson suggest that the permanent employment of dedicated public servants promises a cadre of bureaucrats driven by an ethos of office. Weber describes the distinctive ethos of the bureaucrat as 'impersonal, expert, procedural and hierarchical' (Du Gay 2008, p. 338). Wilson (1887, p. 216) calls for a: 'Steady, hearty allegiance to the policy of the government they serve'. Although largely ignored through much of the twentieth century, the idea that public servants might be motivated by a distinctive ethos emerged as important avenue of public management research in the 1990s.

Perry and Wise define PSM as 'an individual's predisposition to respond to motives grounded primarily or uniquely in public institutions and organizations' (Perry & Wise 1990, p. 368). Perry (1996) suggests a measurement scale which includes items to measure 'commitment to the public interest', 'compassion', 'self-sacrifice' and 'attraction to public policy making'. Although Rainey and Steinbauer (1999, p. 23) define PSM more broadly as a 'general altruistic motivation to serve the interests of a community of people, a state, a nation or humankind', Perry's (1996) approach to the definition and measurement of PSM still dominates the market of empirical studies (Ritz et al. 2016).

Almost all PSM theorists share the presumption first that PSM is higher among public than private employees and second that high levels of PSM are key to explaining the effectiveness of public organisations. Evidence to support these two contentions is given some support in Ritz et al.'s (2016) systematic review of the PSM literature. They find public sector experience to be positively associated with PSM whether because as Awan et al. (2020, p. 620) put it 'individuals with higher levels of PSM are more likely to seek employment in the public sector' or as Pandey and Stazyk (2008) explain, because the public sector will overtime inculcate PSM in those who serve in its ranks. Either way, given the nature of Perry's scale and a shortage of comparative studies of public and private organisations, the association between sector and motivation is deserving of more research.

The PSM performance dividend enjoys a little more support. Theorists hypothesise that increased commitment and engagement of public service motivated individuals will translate into a series of performance benefits. The studies reviewed by Ritz et al. (2016) find PSM to be positively associated with a series of desirable outcomes including individual performance, job satisfaction, organisational commitment, low turnover intention and organisational performance. Awan et al. (2020) add organisation citizenship behaviours – like whistleblowing, collaboration and unpaid over-time – to the list of benefits.

Ritz et al. (2016) are critical, however, of the narrow focus of a literature which is heavily dependent on Perry's definition and scale for PSM measurement. They also make the point that very few of the studies included in their review considered the dark side of PSM (Ritz et al. 2016). Scholars working in this area argue that a misfit between the high motivation of the individual and the constrained context in which they work can lead to a series of problems like stress, dissatisfaction, presentism, absenteeism, burnout and (paradoxically) turnover intention (Schott & Ritz 2018; Awan et al. 2020). While sometimes harmful to the individual employee, PSM can drive organisational dysfunction as well.

Schott and Ritz (2018) suggest that organisational dysfunction may stem from the group think of a strong PSM culture. As they explain, 'individuals belonging to homogeneous groups of highly public-service motivated people are likely to be blindly loyal to the regime and its values' (Schott & Ritz 2018, p. 36). In such a way, PSM may be associated with a resistance to innovation and a reluctance to respond to the changing needs of citizen-consumers. Moynihan (2013) considers a different driver of dysfunction. As he suggests, bureaucrats may perform too well as advocates of their cause. Those who 'sincerely believe in the benefits of their programs' may push for funding levels or service commitments in excess of that desired by citizens (Moynihan 2013, p. 182). In a similar way, a determination to actively represent the interests of one group – or indeed to pursue the goals of a particular programme – may run counter to the traditional virtue of bureaucratic neutrality (Schott & Ritz 2018). Schott and Ritz (2018) use the example of torture by the US military in Abu Ghraib prison to argue that high levels of PSM may lead to so-called noble cause corruption. In cases such as these, well-motivated individuals might come to believe that their commitment to an altruistic end may justify shortcutting or even subverting due process. Ironically then a detailed study of the dysfunctions of PSM takes us back to the problems of corruption that Weber and Wilson took to be answered by the idea of bureaucracy.

It should be said, however, that the bulk of the evidence does not suggest that the dark side of PSM predominates. Ripoll and Breaugh (2019, p. 1529) find that 'when public servants possess motivations reflecting a public service identity it becomes a strong deterrent of tolerance of unethical behaviour'. In practical terms, according to Ritz et al. (2016) managers need to recognise PSM as part of the landscape, using it where they have it and actively fostering it where they do not. Managing PSM also means recognising the circumstances in which PSM may have dysfunctional effects. Ripoll and Breaugh (2019) suggest that a regard to the benefits of PSM should extend to explicit attempts to manage financial stress and job insecurity.

Pursuing this theme, Moynihan (2010, p. 24) considers 'the risks of using a market model – tying contingent pay incentives to performance measures – for public service work'. He suggests that remuneration packages which reward self-interest will see employees more focused on maximising their pay than doing the right thing. Otherwise expressed, extrinsic forms of incentivisation will tend to 'crowd out intrinsic motivations' (Moynihan 2010, p. 27). Reassuringly, Moynihan and Pandey (2007) also find the reverse to be true in that hierarchical organisations which are clearly focused on their mission provide a conducive context for the development of PSM. A finding which sits comfortably with the Weberian vision of hierarchical organisations staffed by public servants selected and remunerated in such a way as to maintain an appropriate ethos of office (Du Gay 2008).

PSM research – like the other themes of bureaucracy considered in this chapter – has come full circle. While earlier work took PSM to be a clearly identifiable individual level phenomenon, distinctive to the public sector with measurable (and overwhelmingly positive) effects, contemporary work asks some more difficult questions. Bozeman and Su (2015) call for the clarification of the distinction between more generic concepts like altruism and PSM. They also call for more work on the independent variables (whether individual or institutional) associated with the development of PSM. O'Leary (2019) looks at the definition of (and influences on) the public at the heart of PSM. In place of individual altruism, a normative approach to the public interest allows for a variety of definitions influenced by a number of institutions. Alongside the rather different definitions of Weber and Perry, the professions emphasise the service to the client and society, while the managers created by the NPM focus on the interests of the organisation. How differences in the definition and representation of these different publics plays out in organisational decision-making remains a fascinating but little illuminated question.

Conclusion

The key themes of bureaucracy introduced by Weber and Wilson have endured into the contemporary study of public administration. Formalisation, accountability, meritocracy, ethos and performance management are as important today as they were at the beginning of the twentieth century. Our interest in these things has changed, however. Whereas Weber and Wilson's approach was largely historical and theoretical, much contemporary research has been orientated to an empirical understanding of the themes they established. We now know much more about how the central planks of bureaucracy work in real organisations.

Following Merton (1936) and Simon's (1944) lead, the lion's share of that empirical work has focused on bureaucracy's many problems. Rather than driving endless improvements in efficiency, formalisation has been blamed for the creation of red tape. Instead of principal agent accountability, researchers now describe a whole series of stakeholders co-producing a variety of accountabilities oriented to the maintenance of their respective reputations. Similarly, research emphasising the functional effects of performance management is at least balanced by work pointing to its susceptibility to gaming and manipulation. Researchers of merit find more and more reasons to question the defence of neutrality in favour of politicisation and active representation. Public service motivation has, until recently, enjoyed a better press, but even here researchers have started to ask some awkward questions about its distinctiveness at the same time as they evidence the manner in which high PSM can backfire on both the individual and the organisation.

While the dysfunctional focus of much contemporary work might be taken as an indictment of bureaucracy, the detail of that work hints at more positive conclusions. In such a way, years of red-tape research have largely failed to find the deadweight drag on performance envisaged by bureaucracy's critics. Performance management, while associated with a variety of gaming behaviours, still seems genuinely to improve performance. The unpacking of accountability and merit underlines the benefits of Weber and Wilson's formulation even if both are hard to realise in practice. PSM research consistently finds an ethos which is positively related to a series of desirable outcomes. Put another way there is an increasing body of evidence that suggests that bureaucracy works. Based on a study of the resources devoted to bureaucracy in UK universities, Andrews et al. (2017, p. 134) go so far as to conclude – in a manner almost inconceivable in preceding decades – that 'big and complex public organizations can benefit from devoting additional resources to administration'.

Despite a century of criticism, this review, like others before it (Thompson & Alvesson 2005), finds bureaucracy in surprisingly good health. Partly this is because its failings have been exaggerated, but it might also be explained by the fact we cannot let go of the rationality and accountability it promises (Olsen 2006). Bureaucracy's persistence may also be attributed, however, to a continual process of adaptation which has updated the themes first introduced by Weber and Wilson. Part of that adaptation has involved the development of hybrid forms of organisation which combine elements of bureaucracy with ideas like autonomy, markets and collaboration. It is to those alternative forms of organisation that this book now turns.

References

Andrews, R., Boyne, G., & Mostafa, A. M. S. (2017). 'When bureaucracy matters for organizational performance: Exploring the benefits of administrative intensity in big and complex organizations'. *Public Administration*, 95(1), 115–139.

Awan, S., Bel, G., & Esteve, M. (2020). 'The benefits of PSM: An oasis or a mirage?'. *Journal of Public Administration Research and Theory*, 30(4), 619–635.

Bach, T., & Veit, S. (2018). 'The determinants of promotion to high public office in Germany: Partisan loyalty, political craft, or managerial competencies?'. *Journal of Public Administration Research and Theory*, 28(2), 254–269.

Behn, R. D. (2003). 'Why measure performance? Different purposes require different measures'. *Public Administration Review*, 63(5), 586–606.

Bevan, G., & Hood, C. (2006). 'What's measured is what matters: Targets and gaming in the English public health care system'. *Public Administration*, 84(3), 517–538.

Blom, R., Borst, R. T., & Voorn, B. (2020). 'Pathology or inconvenience? A meta-analysis of the impact of red tape on people and organizations'. *Review of Public Personnel Administration*. doi: 10.1177/0734371X20924117.

Bovens, M. (1998). *The Quest for Responsibility: Accountability and Citizenship in Complex Organisations.* Cambridge: Cambridge University Press.

Boyne, G. A., & Chen, A. A. (2007). 'Performance targets and public service improvement'. *Journal of Public Administration Research and Theory*, 17(3), 455–477.

Bozeman, B. (1993). 'A theory of government "red tape"'. *Journal of Public Administration Research and Theory*, 3(3), 273–303.

Bozeman, B., & Su, X. (2015). 'Public service motivation concepts and theory: A critique'. *Public Administration Review*, 75(5), 700–710.

Bozeman, B., & Youtie, J. (2020). 'Robotic bureaucracy: Administrative burden and red tape in university research'. *Public Administration Review*, 80(1), 157–162.

Broadbent, J., & Laughlin, R. (2009). 'Performance management systems: A conceptual model'. *Management Accounting Research*, 20(4), 283–295.

Brewer, G. A., & Walker, R. M. (2010a). 'The impact of red tape on governmental performance: An empirical analysis'. *Journal of Public Administration Research and Theory*, 20(1), 233–257.

Brewer, G. A., & Walker, R. M. (2010b). 'Explaining variation in perceptions of red tape: A Professionalism-Marketization model'. *Public Administration*, 88(2), 418–438.

Brewer, G. A., & Walker, R. M. (2012). 'Red tape: The bane of public organizations?'. In Walker, R. M., Boyne, G. A., & Brewer, G. A. (Eds.), *Public Management and Performance: Research Directions*, Cambridge: Cambridge University Press, 110–126.

Buchanan, B. (1975). 'Red-tape and the service ethic: Some unexpected differences between public and private managers'. *Administration & Society*, 6(4), 423–444.

Busuioc, E. M., & Lodge, M. (2016). 'The reputational basis of public accountability'. *Governance*, 29(2), 247–263.

Busuioc, M., & Lodge, M. (2017). 'Reputation and accountability relationships: Managing accountability expectations through reputation'. *Public Administration Review*, 77(1), 91–100.

Christiansen, P. M., Niklasson, B., & Öhberg, P. (2016) 'Does politics crowd out professional competence? The organisation of ministerial advice in Denmark and Sweden'. *West European Politics*, 39, 1230–1250.

Dahlström, C., Lapuente, V., & Teorell, J. (2012). 'The merit of meritocratization: Politics, bureaucracy, and the institutional deterrents of corruption'. *Political Research Quarterly*, 65(3), 656–668.

Dorn, W. L. (1931). 'The Prussian bureaucracy in the eighteenth century'. *Political Science Quarterly*, 46(3), 403–423.

Douglas, M. (1982). *In the Active Voice*. London: Routledge.

Du Gay, P. (2008). '"Without affection or enthusiasm" problems of involvement and attachment in "responsive" public management'. *Organization*, 15(3), 335–353.

Dubnick, M. (2005). 'Accountability and the promise of performance: In search of the mechanisms'. *Public Performance & Management Review*, 28(3), 376–417.

Dunleavy, P. (1995). 'Policy disasters: Explaining the UK's record'. *Public Policy and Administration*, 10(2), 52–70.

Ebinger, F., Veit, S., & Fromm, N. (2019). 'The partisan–professional dichotomy revisited: Politicization and decision-making of senior civil servants'. *Public Administration*, 97(4), 861–876.

Elton, G. R. (1953). *Tudor Revolution in Government*. Cambridge: Cambridge University Press.

Fry, G. K. (1969). 'Some weaknesses in the Fulton report on the British home civil service'. *Political Studies*, 17(4), 484–494.

Gerrish, E. (2016). 'The impact of performance management on performance in public organizations: A meta-analysis'. *Public Administration Review*, 76(1), 48–66.

Greenaway, J. (2004). 'Celebrating Northcote/Trevelyan: Dispelling the myths'. *Public Policy and Administration*, 19(1), 1–14.

Groeneveld, S., & Van de Walle, S. (2010). 'A contingency approach to representative bureaucracy: Power, equal opportunities and diversity'. *International Review of Administrative Sciences*, 76(2), 239–258.

Guriev, S. (2004). 'Red tape and corruption'. *Journal of Development Economics*, 73(2), 489–504.

Hood, C. (1991). 'A public management for all seasons?'. *Public Administration*, 69(1), 3–19.

Hood, C. (2000). *The Art of the State: Culture, Rhetoric, and Public Management*. Oxford: Oxford University Press.

Hood, C. (2012). 'Public management by numbers as a performance-enhancing drug: Two Hypotheses'. *Public Administration Review*, 72(s1), S85–S92.

Hood, C., & Piotrowska, B. (2021). 'Goodhart's Law and the gaming of UK public spending numbers'. *Public Performance & Management Review*, 44(2), 250–271.

Höpfl, H. M. (2006). 'Post-bureaucracy and Weber's "modern" bureaucrat". *Journal of Organizational Change Management*, 19(1), 8–21.

Hupe, P., & Hill, M. (2007). 'Street-level bureaucracy and public accountability'. *Public Administration*, 85(2), 279–299.

Jacobsen, C. B., & Jakobsen, M. L. (2018). 'Perceived organizational red tape and organizational performance in public services'. *Public Administration Review*, 78(1), 24–36.

Kaufman, H. (1956). 'Emerging conflicts in the doctrines of public-administration'. *American Political Science Review*, 50(4), 1057–1073.

Kaufman, H. (1977). *Red Tape: Its Origins, Uses and Abuses*. Washington, DC: Brookings Institution.

Kaufmann, W., & Tummers, L. (2017). 'The negative effect of red tape on procedural satisfaction'. *Public Management Review*, 19(9), 1311–1327.

Kearny, R. C., & Hays, S. W. (1985). 'The politics of selection: Spoils, merit and representative bureaucracy'. In Rosenbloom, D. H. (Ed.), *Public Personnel Policy: The Politics of Civil Service*, Port Washington, NY: Associated Faculty Press, 60–80.

Kopecký, P., Meyer-Sahling, J., Panizza, F., Scherlis, G., Schuster, C., & Spirova, M. (2016). 'Party patronage in contemporary democracies: Results from an expert survey in 22 countries from five regions'. *European Journal of Political Research*, 55, 416–431.

Lim, H. H. (2006). 'Representative bureaucracy: Rethinking substantive effects and active representation'. *Public Administration Review*, 66(2), 193–204.

Marinetto, M. (2011). 'A Lipskian analysis of child protection failures from Victoria Climbié to "Baby P"'. *Public Administration*, 89(3), 1164–1181.

McCann, L., Hassard, J. S., Granter, E., & Hyde, P. J. (2015). 'Casting the lean spell: The promotion, dilution and erosion of lean management in the NHS'. *Human Relations*, 68(10), 1557–1577.

Meier, K. J. (2019). 'Theoretical frontiers in representative bureaucracy: New directions for research'. *Perspectives on Public Management and Governance*, 2(1), 39–56.

Meier, K. J., & Hawes, D. P. (2009). 'Ethnic conflict in France: A case for representative bureaucracy?'. *The American Review of Public Administration*, 39(3), 269–285.

Meier, K. J., & Nicholson-Crotty, J. (2006). 'Gender, representative bureaucracy, and law enforcement: The case of sexual assault'. *Public Administration Review*, 66(6), 850–860.

Merton, R. K. (1936). 'The unanticipated consequences of purposive social action'. *American Sociological Review*, 1(6), 894–904.

Mosher, F. C. (1968). *Democracy and the Public Service*. New York: Oxford University Press.

Moynihan, D. P. (2010). 'A workforce of cynics? The effects of contemporary reforms on public service motivation'. *International Public Management Journal*, 13(1), 24–34.

Moynihan, D. (2013). 'Does public service motivation lead to budget maximisation'. *International Public Management Journal*, 16(2), 179–196.

Moynihan, D. P., & Pandey, S. K. (2007). 'The role of organizations in fostering public service motivation'. *Public Administration Review*, 67(1), 40–53.

O'Leary, C. (2019). 'Public service motivation: a rationalist critique'. *Public Personnel Management*, 48(1), 82–96.

Olsen, J. P. (2006). 'Maybe it is time to rediscover bureaucracy'. *Journal of Public Administration Research and Theory*, 16(1), 1–24.

Osborne, S. P., Radnor, Z., Kinder, T., & Vidal, I. (2015). 'The SERVICE framework: A public-service-dominant approach to sustainable public services'. *British Journal of Management*, 26(3), 424–438.

Pandey, S. K., Coursey, D. H., & Moynihan, D. P. (2007). 'Organizational effectiveness and bureaucratic red tape: A multimethod study'. *Public Performance & Management Review*, 30(3), 398–425.

Pandey, S. K., & Stazyk, E. C. (2008). 'Antecedents and correlates of public service motivation'. In Perry, J. L. & Hondeghem, A. (Eds.), *Motivation in Public Management: The Call of Public Service*, Oxford: Oxford University Press, 101–117.

Panizza, F., Peters, B. G., & Ramos Larraburu, C. R. (2019). 'Roles, trust and skills: A typology of patronage appointments'. *Public Administration*, 97(1), 147–161.

Park, S., & Liang, J. (2020). 'Merit, diversity, and performance: Does diversity management moderate the effect of merit principles on governmental performance?'. *Public Personnel Management*, 49(1), 83–110.

Perry, J. L. (1996). 'Measuring public service motivation: An assessment of construct reliability and validity'. *Journal of Public Administration Research and Theory*, 6(1), 5–22.

Perry, J. L., & Wise, L. R. (1990). 'The motivational bases of public service'. *Public Administration Review*, 50, 367–373.

Peters, B. G., & Pierre, J. (Eds.). (2004). *Politicization of the Civil Service in Comparative Perspective: The Quest for Control*. London/New York: Routledge.

Radnor, Z. J., Holweg, M., & Waring, J. (2012). 'Lean in healthcare: The unfilled promise?'. *Social Science & Medicine*, 74(3), 364–371.

Radnor, Z., & Osborne, S. P. (2013) 'Lean: A failed theory for public services?'. *Public Management Review*, 15(2), 265–287.

Rainey, H. G. (1989). 'Public management: Recent research on the political context and managerial roles, structures, and behaviors'. *Journal of Management*, 15(2), 229–250.

Rainey, H. G., & Steinbauer, P. (1999). 'Galloping elephants: Developing elements of a theory of effective government organizations'. *Journal of Public Administration Research and Theory*, 9(1), 1–32.

Rauch, J. E., & Evans, P. B. (2000). 'Bureaucratic structure and bureaucratic performance in less developed countries'. *Journal of Public Economics*, 75(1), 49–71.

Riccucci, N. M., & Van Ryzin, G. G. (2017). 'Representative bureaucracy: A lever to enhance social equity, coproduction, and democracy'. *Public Administration Review*, 77(1), 21–30.

Ripoll, G., & Breaugh, J. (2019). 'At their wits' end? Economic stress, motivation and unethical judgement of public servants'. *Public Management Review*, 21(10), 1516–1537.

Ritz, A., Brewer, G. A., & Neumann, O. (2016). 'Public service motivation: A systematic literature review and outlook'. *Public Administration Review*, 76(3), 414–426.

Roberts, A. S. (2020). 'Bearing the white man's burden: American empire and the origin of public administration'. *Perspectives on Public Management and Governance*, 3(3), 185–196.

Rourke, F. E. (1992). 'Responsiveness and neutral competence in American bureaucracy'. *Public Administration Review*, 52(6), 539–546.

Sager, F., & Rosser, C. (2009). 'Weber, Wilson, and Hegel: Theories of modern bureaucracy'. *Public Administration Review*, 69(6), 1136–1147.

Seddon, J., & Caulkin, S. (2007) 'Systems thinking, lean production and action learning'. *Action Learning: Research and Practice*, 4(1), 9–24.

Schott, C., & Ritz, A. (2018). 'The dark sides of public service motivation: A multi-level theoretical framework'. *Perspectives on Public Management and Governance*, 1(1), 29–42.

Simon, H. (1944). 'Decision making and administrative organizations'. *Public Administration Review*, 4(1), 16–30.

Stillman, R. J. (1973). 'Woodrow Wilson and the study of administration: A new look at an old essay'. *American Political Science Review*, 67(2), 582–588.

Thelen, K. (2003). 'How institutions evolve: Insights from comparative-historical analysis'. In Mahoney, J. & Rueschemeyer, D. (Eds.), *Comparative Historical Analysis in the Social Sciences*, Cambridge: Cambridge University Press, 208–240.

Thomann, E., Hupe, P., & Sager, F. (2018). 'Serving many masters: Public accountability in private policy implementation'. *Governance*, 31(2), 299–319.

Thompson, P., & Alvesson, M. (2005). 'Bureaucracy at work: Misunderstandings and mixed blessings'. In Du Gay, P. (Ed.), *The Values of Bureaucracy*, Oxford: Oxford University Press, 121–140.

Vigoda, E. (2002). 'From responsiveness to collaboration: Governance, citizens, and the next generation of public administration'. *Public Administration Review*, 62(5), 527–540.

Weber, M. (1978). *Economy and Society: An Outline of Interpretive Sociology*. In Roth, G. & Wittich, C. (Eds.), Berkeley: University of California Press.

Wilson, W. (1887). 'The study of administration'. *Political Science Quarterly*, 2(2), 197–222.

Young, M. D. (1994). *The Rise of the Meritocracy*. New Brunswick, NJ: Transaction Publishers.

3   Autonomy and public management

Alongside an appreciation of the merits of bureaucracy, public management has long relied on the practice of releasing some functions from central management and control (Thynne & Wettenhall 2004). Governments create autonomous institutions when the integrated mechanisms of bureaucracy are seen to be deficient in some way. In this manner, the UK's relatively independent Bank of England was established at the end of the seventeenth century in a bid to enhance 'the credibility of Parliament's promises to repay its debts' (Broz & Grossman 2004, p. 49; North & Weingast 1989). Rainey and Steinbauer (1999) see autonomy as one of the key drivers of public service effectiveness. They propose that: 'Government agencies will be more effective when they have higher levels of autonomy in relation to external stakeholders, but not extremely high levels of autonomy' (Rainey & Steinbauer 1999, p. 16). Egeberg and Trondal (2009, p. 686) describe the push and pull of bureaucratic integration and autonomy enhancing delegation as one of the 'enduring themes of public administration'.

A bundle of different reforms – including devolution, decentralisation, agencification, and delegation – promise to liberate and empower nominally subservient people or organisations with, as Van Thiel (2004, p. 176) puts it, the 'ownership of the rights of production'. At the political-constitutional level this is achieved through devices like federalism and devolution to elected politicians whether they be at the regional, local or even neighbourhood level. Managerial delegation, by contrast, leaves political authority at the centre, but it devolves considerable administrative autonomy to organisations or individuals tasked with the performance of particular functions (Overman 2016). While the promise of administrative delegation led in the first instance to the independence of central banks, more recently the delegation idea has informed the agencification of central government departments and semi-autonomous status for hospitals, schools and a variety of other organisations.

Langfred (2004, p. 385) defines autonomy as the 'freedom and discretion' to carry out an 'assigned' task. Focusing on public management, Groenleer (2014, p. 258) describes it as the freedom 'to act and make decisions relatively unbound by the preferences and interests of the core ministry or parent department'. As with freedom, there are two sides to the autonomy coin (Berlin 1969; Clark 1984; Pratchett 2004; Verhoest et al. 2004). The first points to the need to remove regulations that constrain the organisation. The second focuses on the positive ways in which that liberty might be employed. Of course, neither of these states can be fully realised. No organisation can be entirely freed from constraint any more than it could ever be fully empowered to realise its potential. Egeberg and Trondal (2009, p. 685) conclude that 'the autonomous institution is seldom found; more autonomy gained in one relationship may be followed by more dependence in another'.

Autonomy then, like all the other themes considered in this book, can be realised only in particular dimensions and relative terms (Yesilkagit & Van Thiel 2008). Recognising the complexity of the autonomy idea, Verhoest et al. (2004) identify two enabling senses of the word (policy and managerial autonomy) and four sets of constraints (structural, financial, legal and interventional). Governments tend to increase autonomy in one regard while tightening one or other form of constraint. In such a way, Verhoest (2005) describes the increase in managerial autonomy promised by the new public management as contingent upon the imposition of tighter controls on incentives, competition and performance. The autonomy of the new public management agenda is a precursor – a necessary but not sufficient condition – for the creation of interorganisational competition. Bureaucratic departments cannot be asked to compete – it just does not make any sense – they need first to be turned into standalone organisations. The coincidence of increased autonomy with increased control over outputs and outcomes – the so-called 'paradox of autonomization' (Smullen et al. cited in Groenleer 2014) – makes it difficult to disentangle the effects of liberation from the imposition of new forms of control. Indeed, much of the recent empirical work on autonomy tends to focus more on the effects of a competitive environment or tighter performance management than the freedom from central control.

The case for the delegation and empowerment of inferior units or individuals is informed by a number of lines of reasoning or 'logics of delegation' as Majone (2001) puts it. Distinctions between them blur at the margins and are oftentimes bundled together such that it is impossible to say that any one logic of delegation applies in any one case of reform. Political delegation emphasises a deontological claim that decisions should be made at a particular level or by a particular group of stakeholders. In such a way, the case for devolution in federal style systems is informed more by considerations of the rights of identity than decision-making efficiency (Kay 2003; Pratchett 2004). Merely changing the location of decision-making is, by this logic, in principle the right thing to do. While it may not deliver improved performance, it should still lead to more satisfied local stakeholders.

The case for managerial delegation, in contrast, is largely although not exclusively consequential. Autonomous or independent central banks are claimed to perform better at controlling inflation that their bureaucratically integrated equivalents (Alesina & Summers 1993; Arnone et al. 2009). In the simplest of terms, autonomy promises improved performance. Four distinct lines of argument promise to elaborate this logic. The first, consistent with Verhoest et al.'s (2004) constraint perspective, suggests that performance is improved by removing dysfunctions – like red tape and political interference – which distort neutral decision-making. Second, autonomy should in the positive sense empower some groups, initially professionals and latterly managers to exercise their distinctive competencies. Third, whereas hierarchical systems privilege the voices of those with superior status irrespective of the value of their contribution, autonomy should allow organisations to listen to voices – citizen-consumers and other local stakeholders – which are more germane to core tasks. Fourth and finally, autonomy may prompt a change in the culture of the organisation which sees more motivated managers and employees work harder and more creatively at solving the problems facing them. The next sections look at each of these arguments in turn.

Freedom from bureaucracy and political interference

First and foremost, the prospectus for autonomy promises to shore up the idea of neutral competence by removing distortions from the day-to-day decision-making of subsidiary organisations. Kaufman (1956) argues that the search for neutral competence explains the creation of independent boards and commissions in the US: the so-called headless fourth branch of government. Two types of distortion seem particularly important (Thatcher 2002; Thatcher & Sweet 2002). First are the administrative problems of operating in a larger multifunction bureaucracy. As Kettl (1997, p. 447) explains, reformers 'believed that managers knew the right things to do, but that existing rules, procedures, and structures created barriers to doing it'. Second, autonomy promises freedom from excessive political interference in everyday decision-making.

As was discussed in the preceding chapter the democratic legitimacy of a permanent bureaucracy depends on the idea of a neutrally competent civil service which delivers both responsiveness to politicians and propriety to the public. While neither is easily achieved in isolation, they are certainly not always complementary (West 2005). Political responsiveness may play well with the party in power, but it can all too easily undercut the public's trust in governing institutions which are expected, at least at some level, to stand above and apart from the interests of parties and politicians. But it is not just political interference that damages bureaucracy's reputation for neutral competence. Bureaucracies can damage themselves when formalisation – in the form of regulations, meetings and due diligence – tip into red tape.

By detaching an organisation and function from its bureaucratic and political context, autonomy promises to provide some insulation or freedom from political interference and some protection (or freedom) from everything other than home grown red tape (Overman 2016; Overman & Van Thiel 2016). Van Thiel (2004) describes this insulation as providing a potential saving in coordination costs. In theory at least, insulation from the bureaucratic dysfunctions of red tape and political interference will give (relatively) autonomous organisations the opportunity to be a better bureaucracy with genuinely neutral decision-making at its heart.

First, as we have seen, rules intended to deliver efficiency and effectiveness are subject to dysfunction. While the origins of red tape are numerous, one well established line of argument suggests a positive relationship between pathological formalisation and organisational size (Kaufmann et al. 2019; Ouchi 2006). Otherwise expressed diseconomies of scale emerge because not all of the rules designed in distant parts of the bureaucratic empire will be as functional to task delivery as we might hope. Indeed, the higher and broader the bureaucracy, the greater the coordination burden imposed on each separate function (see Bozeman et al. 1992 for a review). The efficiency of function delivery may then be harmed by red tape imposed by the bureaucracy or the broader environment in which it operates. Delegation to smaller relatively autonomous units of government should in theory free managers from constraints imposed by their parent organisations. The antidote to large size is as Ouchi (2006, p. 299) puts it 'greater decentralization of decision-making authority'.

Empirical confirmation of the red-tape busting qualities of autonomy is not as apparent as might be imagined. On the positive side, Burian-Fitzgerald et al. (2004, p. 29) report that Charter schools in the US 'use their autonomy in staffing policies to recruit a teaching force that is different from the teaching force hired by traditional public schools'. Different, it has to be said, in that they are and markedly 'less likely to be certified, have adequate training in maths, and have 5 or more years of experience', but they are apparently 'more likely to have attended more selective colleges than public school teachers' (Burian-Fitzgerald et al. 2004, p. 29). Supporting these findings, Oberfield (2016, p. 315) reports that teachers in charter schools were 'less likely to experience' red tape and more likely 'to feel autonomous' than teachers in traditional public schools.

As well as removing the shackles of constraint, autonomy promises to protect function delivery from excessive political interference. Although fundamental to democratic accountability, the pivotal position enjoyed by elected politicians gives them the opportunity to involve themselves in the day-to-day processes of service delivery. Whether for reasons of nepotism, naked self-interest or just 'temporal inconsistency' (Verhoest et al. 2004, p. 102), political interference may on occasion conflict with the tenets of objective and independent decision-making we expect of bureaucracy (Overman 2016, p. 1246).

It is not just day-to-day delivery which needs to be protected from political interference. Kleizen et al. (2018) point to the importance of stability in the development of autonomy. Frequent reorganisation makes it difficult to develop specialised knowledge at the same time as it distracts from the maintenance of long-term relationships. Furthermore, a history of structural reorganisation acts as a threat of further reform in such a way as to encourage managers to act 'in a relatively risk averse manner' (Kleizen et al. 2018, p. 360). Bearing this out, Kleizen et al. (2018, p. 359) study of 44 Flemish organisations find 'the more turbulent an organization's structural reform history, the less likely it is to have a higher than average degree of strategic policy autonomy'.

In a longitudinal study of Norwegian agencies, Egeberg and Trondal (2009, pp. 684–685) find that: 'Officials within Ministerial departments are significantly more sensitive to signals from executive politicians than their counterparts within national agencies'. They go on to conclude that agencification may 'mute signals from the political leadership and to some extent insulate professional considerations from political concerns' (Egeberg & Trondal 2009, p. 685). In such a way, they reckon (Egeberg & Trondal 2009, p. 868) that autonomy provided by agencification 'may safeguard more equal treatment of individual cases across time regardless of shifting ministers of various political colors'. Christensen and Lægreid (2007, p. 515) concur, arguing that increases in autonomy limit 'cabinet members' leeway for political discretion and control' although they go on to observe that in specific instances the political leaders can still interfere in a bid to reassert control.

As is often the case in public management, however, not everything is as it seems. Delegation to autonomous agencies has, as McNamara (2002, p. 48) explains, 'important legitimising and symbolic properties'. The poor reputation of public bureaucracies is such that the simple act of delegating 'decision-making competencies' to *apparently* autonomous agencies promises to 'enhance the credibility of government policies' (Verhoest et al. 2004, p. 102). As Van Thiel and Yesilkagit (2011, p. 785) put it: 'Delegating a public task to an agent will increase the credibility of the principal's policy commitment, as there will be fewer possibilities for (political) interference and lower risks of partiality or partisanship'. Delegation has the further merit that when policies disappoint, politicians will be insulated to some degree from the blame that might otherwise come home to roost. Overman's (2017, p. 223) particularly rigorous study of the relationship between autonomous organisation and citizen satisfaction in 15 European Countries, finds some support for this protective effect in that: 'Semi-autonomous tax authorities absorb some of the blame for bad performance'.

The popularity of reforms promising to reduce red tape and political interference give politicians good reason to institute the appearance of autonomy enhancing reforms while continuing to regulate and interfere in the normal hierarchical manner. This means, as Bach (2018) observes, that while a formal grant of autonomy 'does sometimes affect actual autonomy' the relationship is not as straightforward as it appears. Bach and Jann (2010, p. 461) also question the unlocking the shackles argument when they conclude that in Germany 'federal agencies do not enjoy the kind of managerial freedom that is commonly associated with an ideal-typical, modern agency'. Yesilkagit and Van Thiel's (2008, p. 151) study of Dutch autonomous agencies leads them to conclude the 'the level of formal autonomy is not a straightforward indicator of the level of actual or de facto autonomy'. Organisations which are closest to their political principals sometimes have more autonomy than those which are more detached (Yesilkagit & Van Thiel, 2008). Reflecting on a close reading of the changing policy framework of the UK's executive agencies, Elston (2014, p. 459) concludes that 'the original emphasis on managerial empowerment, devolution and de-politicization' has since been 'replaced by counter-themes of ministerial control and centralization'.

Freedom for professional and managerial judgement

It is perhaps not surprising that the negative dimension of autonomy – in terms of freedom from red tape or political interference – has proved difficult to verify. In place of the 'freedom from' approach, the 'freedom to' perspective focuses on the positive changes associated with the grant of autonomy (Berlin 1969). Professionalisation projects provide a case in point. In return for guarantees of training and self-regulation, the state recognises professional groups by granting them 'production rights' (Van Thiel 2004) in particular service areas. The grant of autonomy makes a virtue of the 'substantial information asymmetries' between the lay political principals and their expert agents (Ossege 2015, p. 110). While the professions get the right to control their work, the state enjoys a significant saving in the transaction costs that would result from hierarchical or market form of delivery.

Crucially, professional decision-making is very different to bureaucratic decision-making. Whereas the bureaucrat follows principles 'without affection or enthusiasm' (Du Gay 2008), the professional is asked to apply their expertise in the interest of their client. While it empowers the professional, it also allows for the provision of bespoke services which are anathema to bureaucratic principles. Professionalisation (even when combined in some way with bureaucracy) marks a significant departure from the strictly bureaucratic form of administration (Kearney & Sinha 1988).

The promise of this idea lay behind the huge growth of the professions and their domination of the policy process in technocratic policy communities apparent through much of the twentieth century (Laffin 1986). As Perkin explains:

> What was new in the twentieth century was the belief that most social problems, not just the obvious ones like sanitation and water supply, were the products of social organisation rather than individual inadequacy. Problems thus defined as institutional and societal rather than moral and individual cried out for collective, professional solutions rather than moral discipline and exhortation. And once the legislative and administrative treatment began, the process of professionalisation and feedback set in, by which the welfare professionals uncovered new problems which demanded further legislative and administrative solutions and the recruitment of still more welfare professionals.
>
> (Perkin 1989, pp. 356–357)

While at its height, the pace of professionalisation prompted some commentators to forecast the professionalisation of everyone (Haug 1988), the heady days of professional empowerment proved relatively short lived.

Whether because of a turn to neo-liberalism, fiscal stress or the emergence of new forms of control, much of the empirical work from the 1960s describes the decline of professional autonomy in the face of an increasing tide of bureaucratisation. Scott's study of bureaucratic professionals (Scott 1965, p. 70) found them complaining of 'too much time filling out the various forms required by agency procedures'. His respondents claimed that 'their professional function was rather severely constrained by the administrative and legal framework within which they were required to operate'. Based on survey data from a variety of occupational groups, Hall (1968, p. 102) too finds an inverse relationship between professionalisation and bureaucratisation suggesting indeed that 'increased bureaucratisation threatens professional autonomy'. So strong was the new consensus that in place of the optimism of the preceding decade, Haug (1988) went on to claim that the squeeze on professional autonomy threatened the deprofessionalisation of everyone. More recent work suggests a more complex or varied picture. While frontline professionals may have seen new constraints on their discretion, those prepared to assume managerial or regulatory responsibilities have fared rather better (Kitchener 2000; Laffin 2018).

In place of the period of professionalisation described by Perkin (1989), the new public management of the late twentieth century heralded a rather different empowerment project which promised, as Kettl (1997) put it, 'to let managers manage'. Rather than the individual empowerment associated with professionalisation, the freedom to manage was to be delivered at the organisation level – in hospitals, schools and central government agencies – through a bag of reforms inspired by the notion that 'governments should operate more akin to private sector businesses in order to be efficient and effective' (Kleizen et al. 2018, p. 349).

In a survey of public managers across Europe, Bezes and Jeannot (2018, p. 16) found a positive correlation between the adoption of NPM style reforms (like strategic planning, performance appraisal, benchmarking) and manager perceptions of autonomy. Their data suggest, as they put it, that the 'let managers manage' project identified by Kettl (1997) 'was actually implemented through public management reforms'. Alongside some outlier cases (including Germany and the UK), the Netherlands and the Scandinavian countries exhibited high NPM and high autonomy, whereas central and South Europe (Austria,

France, Spain, Portugal and Italy) exhibited lower engagement with NPM and lower levels of autonomy.

The sequence of these events can be seen clearly in the UK's NHS which – on the basis of a report written by the prominent businessman Roy Griffiths – moved from a profession-based model of collegiate or consensus decision-making (Harrison 1982) to the installation and empowerment of general managers (Pollitt et al. 1991). Asked to juggle 'predetermined targets', 'tightly constrained financial resources' and the medical professions continued defence of its remaining turf, the grant of autonomy should not be exaggerated (Hoque et al. 2004, p. 370). Pollitt et al. (1991, p. 80) were surely right to say initially at least that 'the frontier of control shifted only slightly in favour of management'. That said, 30 years later it is clear that the change of focus from professional to managerial empowerment, heralded by the Griffiths report, was an important one (Gorsky 2013).

While the rise of the new managerial class is readily apparent in the NHS and other public service organisations, it is not immediately clear what it means. The bureaucrat administers the will of their political principal and the professional serves their client and society, but who or what were the newly empowered managers supposed to serve? Part of the answer lies in differences in their sphere of competence. Management, at least of the form prescribed by new public management, is focused on the performance of the organisation. As we have seen, much of the enthusiasm for management stemmed from a rather vague belief in the superiority of private sector techniques focused on the performance and efficiency of the organisation. In the UK at least, private sector managers (in the form of Derek Rayner, Colin Ibbs and Roy Griffiths) were called in to advise central government on the best ways of transferring these techniques into the public sector. All of those techniques presumed, at least in the first instance, the identification of an organisation that could be managed. The empowerment of managers was, as Brunsson and Sahlin-Anderson (2000, p. 736) put it, part of an attempt to create more complete organisation with clear boundaries, identities and objectives.

Freedom to engage with citizens and consumers

While as we have seen a concern for efficiency and performance management provided much of the inspiration for the introduction of general managers into the UK's NHS, managers were intended to promote the voice of the consumer as well. Hitherto the organisation of health care gave priority to bureaucratic and professional voices over those of patients and their representatives. Freed, at least partially, from these structures, the new band of general managers would – so Roy Griffiths, the architect of managerialisation in the UK's NHS, believed – listen to and promote the voice of patients (Pollitt et al. 1991).

Writing of the US Charter school movement, Flanders (2017) appeals to the same logic in suggesting that autonomy should 'shift the power in schools away from the bureaucracy and administration towards parents and teachers'. With fewer bureaucratic hoops to negotiate, Flanders (2017) claims that decentralised organisations 'have a better ability to match the service needs of their constituents'. This, according to Hanushek et al. (2013, p. 1), is the 'prime argument favoring decentralization'. 'Local decision-makers', as they go on to explain:

> have better understanding of the capacity of their schools and the demands that are placed on them by varying student populations. This knowledge in turn permits them to make better resource decisions, to improve the productivity of the schools, and to meet the varying demands of their local constituents.
>
> (Hanushek et al. 2013, p. 1)

Surveying the changes associated with the new public management, Kettl suggests that the idea of 'serving citizens instead of the needs of the bureaucracy' (1997, p. 447) was 'at the core of the let the managers manage' movement.

There are a number of reasons to think that decentralised or autonomous organisations may afford greater opportunities for citizen/consumer engagement than the larger (and more centralised) alternative. The arguments of democratic theorists developed over literally thousands of years suggests that an engagement bonus might operate at three reinforcing levels (Andrews et al. 2019). First of all, small size and proximity serve to boost citizen efficacy through a local issues and local people effect. Briefly stated, citizens are more inclined, and more confident of their capacity to engage successfully with the local issues which directly affect their lives than the high politics debated at the national level. Decentralisation also helps citizens develop and then utilise the close community ties developed in local communities. In more theoretical terms, small numbers reduce heterogeneity and the associated 'costs of collective action and cooperation' (Rodriguez-Pose et al. 2009, p. 2043) by making it easier to communicate, develop shared values, and foster the sense of reciprocity, which underpin political efficacy.

Second the act of decentralisation creates new access points for citizens both individually and collectively to engage with authoritative decision-makers. Dahl (1967, p. 957) made the point that 'as the number of citizens increases the proportion who can participate directly in discussions with their top leaders must necessarily grow smaller and smaller'. In the opposite way decentralisation increases the opportunities for citizens to engage with top leaders. As Spina (2014, p. 451) puts it 'an additional level of government simply generates more public officials and increases the chance of interaction between political actors and citizens'. Those decision-makers may by virtue of their new-found autonomy and responsibilities prove more receptive to local and specialised voices than their centralised equivalents could ever afford to be.

Finally, alongside advantages in efficacy and engagement, public choice theorists suggest that small governments will be better able to offer bespoke policies and services to the local population (Boyne 1998; Oates 1999). As Rodriguez-Pose et al. (2009, p. 2043) explain, smaller governments can provide a more fine-grained 'tailoring of policies to local preferences' and, therefore, perform better than their larger counterparts. Where services are more closely matched to the preferences of citizens, so the argument goes, they might well be more satisfied with their government's performance and more inclined to feel that they are able to influence decisions (Kelleher & Lowery 2009). In such a way, a virtuous cycle of increased opportunities and responsiveness provides positive feedback to the development of increased citizen efficacy.

Empirical work largely supports the theorised engagement advantages of small, decentralised governments. Aside from voter turnout (which generally favours larger governments) research across the world points to the participation advantages of small size (Andrews et al. 2019). In a recent study, Fatke (2016, p. 682) finds that 'regional self-rule increases some more demanding and less common forms of participation' such as working in parties, contacting politicians, boycotting and consumer participation. Hefetz and Warner's (2012) study of procurement decisions in US local governments lends support to the idea that it is the professional managers who are particularly sensitive to citizen interests. As they explain it is those governments with professional managers which 'are more likely to recognize the importance of citizen interests' (Hefetz & Warner 2012, p. 307).

Away from work on local governments, the evidence base is more mixed. Egeberg and Trondal (2009, p. 687) find that staff working in relatively autonomous agencies – of the type recommended by Thatcher's private sector advisor Colin Ibbs – 'emphasize user and client interests more than their counterparts within ministerial departments'. Indeed, they go so far as to claim that officials 'rank such concerns higher than a steer from their political masters' (Egeberg & Trondal 2009, p. 687). In a study of 49 Flemish agencies, Wynen and Verhoest (2015) find personnel autonomy (control over salary, promotion and evaluation) to be positively correlated with customer-oriented culture which they measure by emphasis on quality, meeting customer expectations, valuing customers and customer relations. Neshkova's (2014, p. 72) study of budget setting in transport and environment protection agencies in 50 US states, finds that 'agencies with greater autonomy' over budgeting processes 'are more likely to seek public input to inform their budget decisions'. However, Overman's (2017, p. 224) study of citizen satisfaction in 15 European Countries provides 'no statistically significant differences in the satisfaction with service delivery between semi-autonomous agencies and government units'.

Freedom for entrepreneurialism and innovation

The final case for autonomy considered in this chapter turns on the suggestion that relatively autonomous organisations will be more entrepreneurial and innovative. This might partly stem from their freedom from formal procedures which make it difficult to do things differently but at the same time it may be the product of a different culture in the autonomous organisation which is conducive to innovation. While empirical support for the escape from red-tape hypothesis is thin on the ground, evidence of a more developed consumer orientation suggests that the cultural hypothesis may prove more fruitful.

In an important reading of the new public management reforms, Brunsson and Sahlin-Andersson (2000) suggest that the rag bag of policies unleashed on the public sector across the world at the end of the twentieth century were in essence focused on the creation of more complete organisations. Strangely, in some ways, bureaucracies are not really organisations in the contemporary sense of the word. They are merely instrumental mechanisms for the fulfilment of the principal's wish (whether democratically elected or not). According to constitutional tradition at least, bureaucratic agents in the UK get their authority from their political principal whether that be the council (or committee) in local government or the respective minister in the case of UK central government. Because the bureaucrat does nothing more than implement the intent of their political masters, the traditional doctrine of ministerial responsibility dictates that accountability resides with that principal (Barberis 1998). Public sector organisations in the sense that we currently understand them (whether they be agencies, non-departmental bodies, schools or hospitals) did not really exist until reforms associated with the new public management equipped them with attributes of complete organisations (Brunsson & Sahlin-Andersson 2000).

The new organisations of the public sector looked much more like their private sector equivalents than the old bureaucracies of the past. Together with their new general managers they had catchy names, logos, strategies, annual reports, control of human resources, performance management and crucially corporate responsibility. All of these depended as Brunsson and Sahlin-Andersson (2000) point out, on clear organisational boundaries that distinguished them from the traditional bureaucracies at the heart of government. Greer and Hoggett (1999) focus in particular on the displacement of policy with strategy. While bureaucracies implemented the policies developed by their principals, the newly autonomous and complete organisations of the new public management had the freedom to develop strategies. As Greer and Hoggett (1999) explain, strategic thinking emphasises the importance of corporate survival and growth in a competitive environment. Although an anathema to traditional notions of accountability and the cause of celebrated tensions between the responsibility of ministers and managers (Barberis 1998), the new approach was intended to unleash a more entrepreneurial and innovative culture.

Well established literatures in private sector management make the case that strategic autonomy is key to the development and maintenance of an entrepreneurial orientation. Lumpkin et al. (2009, p. 49), high-profile advocates of the case, argue that 'autonomy encourages innovation, promotes the launching of entrepreneurial ventures, and increases the competitiveness and effectiveness of firms'. Wynen et al. (2014, p. 46) explain that the new public management extended this logic to public sector organisations in the hope 'that an increase in managerial autonomy' would 'stimulate a more innovation-oriented culture' and ultimately an improvement in performance. While public sector evidence of the relationship between entrepreneurial cultures and performance remains thin on the ground (Swann 2017), an increasing body of evidence lends support to the idea that autonomy is indeed positively associated with risk taking and innovation.

Kim (2010) defines public sector entrepreneurship in terms of risk taking, innovativeness and proactiveness. He hypothesises that while hierarchy and formalisation are inimical to entrepreneurship, managerial autonomy, alongside a bag of other variables, should stimulate a proactive culture of risk-taking and innovation. Based on a survey of state government departments in the US, Kim (2010, p. 802) finds, consistent with prior research, that 'empowering employees by increasing autonomy and participatory decision making is important in adopting risk-taking and innovative tendencies'. Wynen et al. (2014) argue that autonomous agencies will have both the opportunity and incentive to differentiate themselves from the culture of their parent departments. In place of the traditional cultures of bureaucratic compliance, Wynen et al. (2014, p. 49) expect to see cultures focused on 'on customer-orientation, flexibility, innovation and risk-taking behaviour'. Bearing this out, their survey evidence from five countries suggests that: 'High financial management autonomy' and 'high personnel management autonomy ... each proved independently to have strong positive effects on innovation-oriented culture' (Wynen et al. 2014, pp. 57–59).

Van Thiel and van der Wal's (2010) comparative study of the values of Dutch ministries and their agencies also points to the development of different cultures. They found that the agencies exhibited significantly different ratings of business-like qualities such as serviceability, profitability, sustainability and innovativeness. Based on an analysis of 169 surveys from Dutch municipally owned corporations, Voorn et al. (2020) find that while autonomy of itself does not improve organisational performance, the adoption of a variety of business techniques – like planning, performance management, devolved autonomy, and the development of new products and services – do. Indeed, techniques such as these are 'both directly helpful for performance ... and (partially) mediate the relationship between managerial autonomy and performance' (Voorn et al. 2020, p. 11). They recommend that 'corporatization should not be a goal, but rather a means to introduce business techniques into public service delivery' (Voom et al. 2020, p. 11).

Finally, evidence that the different cultures authorised by autonomy might translate into a greater capacity for innovation comes from Bernier and Deschamps (2020, p. 285) study of the Canadian innovative management awards. Surveying data from the awards process over a twenty-nine-year period they find that 'autonomous organizations tend to be finalists and winners more often than other types of public organization'. They conclude that while agencification may have created 'new problems of coordination', it does indeed appear 'to have been a way to foster innovation' (Bernier & Deschamps 2020, p. 289).

Conclusions

Although prominent in public management for many years, autonomy has proved a difficult form of organisation to research. It is not clear what dimensions of autonomy are most important (policy, finance, human resources), how it should be defined (whether in terms of formal or informal institutional arrangements) or what constraints (whether in terms of red tape or political interference) really make the difference (Ladner et al. 2019). Many of these difficulties stem from the challenge of establishing the absence of hierarchical control. The challenge is compounded, however, by the tendency for autonomy-type reforms to be combined with new disciplinary devices. The new public management, in particular, imposed results-based forms of performance management at the same time as it promised managers the freedom to manage.

The research challenge is made more difficult still by autonomy's reputation as one of the good guys in the landscape of institutional reform. Like partnership, but unlike bureaucracy and marketisation, promises of independence or autonomy are attractive to voters and other stakeholders. Precisely because bureaucracy's reputation has been damaged by the association with political interference and red tape, reforms which purport to shore up independence and neutrality promise a political dividend. Politicians have good reasons then to promise (or even formally adopt) autonomy-type reforms even as they try (perhaps informally) to maintain or even reassert hierarchical control.

Despite these sources of confusion, an accumulating body of evidence suggests that autonomy is associated with a number of positive consequences. While public management researchers cannot yet point to the performance effects showcased in the study of independent central banks (Alesina & Summers 1993; Arnone et al. 2009), they have uncovered evidence of decreasing political interference; the empowerment of key occupational groups; increased engagement with citizen-consumers; and an increased appetite for entrepreneurialism and innovation. There are of course problems as well. A determination to focus on core business and cut the costs of coordination might make autonomous organisations reluctant to collaborate (Bjurstrøm 2021) and more dependent on resources in their local environment (Sholderer 2017).

The promise of 'output legitimacy' which sees agencies deliver superior performance in exchange for autonomy from central control sits uncomfortably, however, with 'the traditional model of parliamentary accountability' (Thatcher & Sweet 2002, p. 18). High-profile squabbles between UK ministers and their agency managers in one regard (Barberis 1998) and complaints of disappearing accountability in another (Hammond et al. 2019) attest to the fragility of this arrangement. Although providing for a relatively simple rebalancing of accountabilities (from inputs to outputs) there are, as Thatcher and

Sweet (2002, p. 19) explain, 'winners and losers' from these reforms. As we have seen, autonomy weakens the ability of representative politicians to interfere in the day-to-day operations of their agencies, at the same time as it empowers agency officials and strengthens the direct lines of accountability to citizen-consumers and other stakeholders.

The balance of these accountabilities will be perceived in markedly different ways depending upon party control, the salience of the issue and other contextual factors. It is for this reason, as Thatcher (2002, p. 136) puts it, that 'there is no automatic link between functional advantages of delegation' and the actual decision to grant autonomy. Differences in contextual factors explain the changing political calculation of the merits of autonomy both between and within countries. They also explain why the push and pull of bureaucratic integration and autonomy are, as Egeberg and Trondal (2009, p. 686) put it, such 'enduring themes of public administration'.

References

Alesina, A., & Summers, L. H. (1993). 'Central bank independence and macroeconomic performance: Some comparative evidence'. *Journal of Money, Credit and Banking*, 25(2), 151–162.

Arnone, M., Laurens, B. J., Segalotto, J. F., & Sommer, M. (2009). 'Central bank autonomy: Lessons from global trends'. *IMF Staff Papers*, 56(2), 263–296.

Andrews, R., Entwistle, T., & Guarneros-Meza, V. (2019). 'Local government size and political efficacy: Do citizen panels make a difference?'. *International Journal of Public Administration*, 42(8), 664–676.

Bach, T. (2018). 'Administrative autonomy of public organizations'. In A. Farazmand (Ed.), *Global Encyclopedia of Public Administration, Public Policy, and Governance*, Springer, 1–9.

Bach, T., & Jann, W. (2010). 'Animals in the administrative zoo: Organizational change and agency autonomy in Germany'. *International Review of Administrative Sciences*, 76(3), 443–468.

Barberis, P. (1998). 'The new public management and a new accountability'. *Public Administration*, 76(3), 451–470.

Berlin, I. (1969). *Four Essays on Liberty*. Oxford: Clarendon Press.

Bernier, L., & Deschamps, C. (2020). 'Autonomy and distance from the centre as drivers of innovation in the public sector: Testing a positioning-based hypothesis'. *Canadian Public Administration*, 63(2), 271–292.

Bezes, P., & Jeannot, G. (2018). 'Autonomy and managerial reforms in Europe: Let or make public managers manage?'. *Public Administration*, 96(1), 3–22.

Bjurstrøm, K. H. (2021). 'How interagency coordination is affected by agency policy autonomy'. *Public Management Review*, 23(3), 397–421.

Boyne, G. A. (1998). *Public Choice Theory and Local Government: A Comparative Analysis of the UK and the USA*. Houndmills: Macmillan.

Bozeman, B., Reed, P. N., & Scott, P. (1992). 'Red tape and task delays in public and private organizations'. *Administration & Society*, 24(3), 290–322.

Broz, J. L., & Grossman, R. S. (2004). 'Paying for privilege: The political economy of Bank of England Charters, 1694–1844'. *Explorations in Economic History*, 41(1), 48–72.

Brunsson, N., & Sahlin-Andersson, K. (2000). 'Constructing organizations: The example of public sector reform'. *Organization Studies*, 21(4), 721–746.

Burian-Fitzgerald, M., Luekens, M. T., & Strizek, G. A. (2004). 'Less red tape or more green teachers: Charter school autonomy and teacher qualifications'. In Bulkely, K. & Wohlstetter, P. (Eds.), *Taking Account of Charter Schools*, New York: Teachers College Press, 11–31.

Christensen, T., & Lægreid, P. (2007). 'Regulatory agencies—The challenges of balancing agency autonomy and political control'. *Governance*, 20(3), 499–520.

Clark, G. L. (1984). 'A theory of local autonomy'. *Annals of the Association of American Geographers*, 74(2), 195–208.

Dahl, R. A. (1967). 'The city in the future of local democracy'. *American Political Science Review*, 61(4), 953–970.

Du Gay, P. (2008). '"Without affection or enthusiasm" problems of involvement and attachment in "responsive" public management'. *Organization*, 15(3), 335–353.

Egeberg, M., & Trondal, J. (2009). 'Political leadership and bureaucratic autonomy: Effects of agencification'. *Governance*, 22(4), 673–688.

Elston, T. (2014). 'Not so "arm's length": Reinterpreting agencies in UK central government'. *Public Administration*, 92(2), 458–476.

Fatke, M. (2016). 'Participatory effects of regional authority: Decentralisation and political participation in comparative perspective'. *West European Politics*, 39(4), 667–687.

Flanders, W. (2017). 'Bang for the buck: Autonomy and charter school efficiency in Milwaukee'. *Journal of School Choice*, 11(2), 282–297.

Gorsky, M. (2013). '"Searching for the people in charge": Appraising the 1983 Griffiths NHS management inquiry'. *Medical History*, 57(1), 87–107.

Greer, A., & Hoggett, P. (1999). 'Public policies, private strategies and local public spending bodies'. *Public Administration*, 77(2), 235–256.

Groenleer, M. L. (2014). 'Agency autonomy actually: Managerial strategies, legitimacy, and the early development of the European Union's agencies for drug and food safety regulation'. *International Public Management Journal*, 17(2), 255–292.

Hall, R. (1968). 'Professionalization and bureaucratization'. *American Sociological Review*, 33(1), 92–104.

Hammond, J., Speed, E., Allen, P., McDermott, I., Coleman, A., & Checkland, K. (2019). 'Autonomy, accountability, and ambiguity in arm's-length metagovernance: The case of NHS England'. *Public Management Review*, 21(8), 1148–1169.

Hanushek, E. A., Link, S., & Woessmann, L. (2013). 'Does school autonomy make sense everywhere? Panel estimates from Pisa'. *Journal of Development Economics*, 104, 212–232.

Harrison, S. (1982). 'Consensus decision-making in the National Health Service'. *Journal of Management Studies*, 19(4), 377–394.

Haug, M. R. (1988). 'A re-examination of the hypothesis of physician de-professionalization'. *The Milbank Quarterly*, 66, 48–56.

Hefetz, A., & Warner, M. E. (2012). 'Contracting or public delivery? The importance of service, market, and management characteristics'. *Journal of Public Administration Research and Theory*, 22(2), 289–317.

Hoque, K., Davis, S., & Humphreys, M. (2004). 'Freedom to do what you are told: Senior management team autonomy in an NHS acute trust'. *Public Administration*, 82(2), 355–375.

Kaufman, H. (1956). 'Emerging conflicts in the doctrines of public-administration'. *American Political Science Review*, 50(4), 1057–1073.

Kaufmann, W., Borry, E. L., & DeHart-Davis, L. (2019). 'More than pathological formalization: Understanding organizational structure and red tape'. *Public Administration Review*, 79(2), 236–245.

Kay, A. (2003). 'Evaluating devolution in Wales'. *Political Studies*, 51(1), 51–66.

Kearney, R. C., & Sinha, C. (1988). 'Professionalism and bureaucratic responsiveness: Conflict or compatibility?'. *Public Administration Review*, 48, 571–579.

Kelleher, C. A., & Lowery, D. (2009). 'Central city size, metropolitan institutions and political participation'. *British Journal of Political Science*, 39(1), 59–92.

Kettl, D. F. (1997). 'The global revolution in public management: Driving themes, missing links'. *Journal of Policy Analysis and Management*, 16(3), 446–462.

Kim, Y. (2010). 'Stimulating entrepreneurial practices in the public sector: The roles of organizational characteristics'. *Administration & Society*, 42(7), 780–814.

Kitchener, M. (2000). 'The bureaucratization of professional roles: The case of clinical directors in UK hospitals'. *Organization*, 7(1), 129–154.

Kleizen, B., Verhoest, K., & Wynen, J. (2018). 'Structural reform histories and perceptions of organizational autonomy: Do senior managers perceive less strategic policy autonomy when faced with frequent and intense restructuring?'. *Public Administration*, 96(2), 349–367.

Ladner, A., Keuffer, N., Baldersheim, H., Hlepas, N., Swianiewicz, P., Steyvers, K., & Navarro, C. (2019). *Patterns of Local Autonomy in Europe*. London: Palgrave Macmillan.

Laffin, M. (1986). *Professionalism and Policy: The Role of the Professions in the Central-Local Government Relationship*. Farnham: Gower.

Laffin, M. (Ed.). (2018). *Beyond Bureaucracy? The Professions in the Contemporary Public Sector*. Abingdon: Routledge.

Langfred, C. W. (2004). 'Too much of a good thing? Negative effects of high trust and individual autonomy in self-managing teams'. *Academy of Management Journal*, 47(3), 385–399.

Lumpkin, G. T., Cogliser, C. C., & Schneider, D. R. (2009). 'Understanding and measuring autonomy: An entrepreneurial orientation perspective'. *Entrepreneurship Theory and Practice*, 33(1), 47–69.

Majone, G. (2001). 'Two logics of delegation: Agency and fiduciary relations in EU governance'. *European Union Politics*, 2(1), 103–122.

McNamara, K. (2002). 'Rational fictions: Central bank independence and the social logic of delegation'. *West European Politics*, 25(1), 47–76.

Neshkova, M. I. (2014). 'Does agency autonomy foster public participation?'. *Public Administration Review*, 74(1), 64–74.

North, D. C., & Weingast, B. R. (1989). 'Constitutions and commitment: The evolution of institutions governing public choice in seventeenth-century England'. *Journal of Economic History*, 49(4), 803–832.

Oates, W. (1999). 'An essay on fiscal federalism'. *Journal of Economic Literature*, 37(3), 1120–1149.

Oberfield, Z. W. (2016). 'A bargain half fulfilled: Teacher autonomy and accountability in traditional public schools and public charter schools'. *American Educational Research Journal*, 53(2), 296–323.

Ossege, C. (2015). 'Driven by expertise and insulation? The autonomy of European regulatory agencies'. *Politics and Governance*, 3(1), 101–113.

Ouchi, W. G. (2006). 'Power to the principals: Decentralization in three large school districts'. *Organization Science*, 17(2), 298–307.

Overman, S. (2016). 'Great expectations of public service delegation: A systematic review'. *Public Management Review*, 18(8), 1238–1262.

Overman, S. (2017). 'Autonomous agencies, happy citizens? Challenging the satisfaction claim'. *Governance*, 30(2), 211–227.

Overman, S., & van Thiel, S. (2016). 'Agencification and public sector performance: A systematic comparison in 20 countries'. *Public Management Review*, 18(4), 611–635.

Perkin, H. (1989). *The Rise of Professional Society: England since 1880*. London: Routledge.

Pollitt, C., Harrison, S., Hunter, D. J., & Marnoch, G. (1991). 'General management in the NHS: The initial impact 1983–88'. *Public Administration*, 69(1), 61–83.

Pratchett, L. (2004). 'Local autonomy, local democracy and the "new localism"'. *Political Studies*, 52(2), 358–375.

Rainey, H. G., & Steinbauer, P. (1999). 'Galloping elephants: Developing elements of a theory of effective government organizations'. *Journal of Public Administration Research and Theory*, 9(1), 1–32.

Rodriguez-Pose, A., Tijmstra, S. A. R., & Bwire, A. (2009). 'Fiscal decentralisation, efficiency, and growth'. *Environment and Planning A*, 41(9), 2041–2062.

Scott, W. R. (1965). 'Reactions to supervision in a heteronomous professional organization'. *Administrative Science Quarterly*, 10, 65–81.

Sholderer, O. (2017). 'Making education work: School autonomy and performance'. *East European Quarterly*, 45(1–2), 27–56.

Spina, N. (2014). 'Decentralisation and political participation: An empirical analysis in Western and Eastern Europe'. *International Political Science Review*, 35(4), 448–462.

Swann, W. L. (2017). 'Modelling the relationship between entrepreneurial orientation, organizational integration, and programme performance in local sustainability'. *Public Management Review*, 19(4), 542–565.

Thatcher, M. (2002). 'Delegation to independent regulatory agencies: Pressures, functions and contextual mediation'. *West European Politics*, 25(1), 125–147.

Thatcher, M., & Sweet, A. S. (2002). 'Theory and practice of delegation to non-majoritarian institutions'. *West European Politics*, 25(1), 1–22.

Thynne, I., & Wettenhall, R. (2004). 'Public management and organizational autonomy: The continuing relevance of significant earlier knowledge'. *International Review of Administrative Sciences*, 70(4), 609–621.

Van Thiel, S. (2004). 'Trends in the public sector: Why politicians prefer quasi-autonomous organizations'. *Journal of Theoretical Politics*, 16(2), 175–201.

Van Thiel, S., & van der Wal, Z. (2010). 'Birds of a feather? The effect of organizational value congruence on the relationship between ministries and quangos'. *Public Organization Review*, 10(4), 377–397.

Van Thiel, S., & Yesilkagit, K. (2011). 'Good neighbours or distant friends? Trust between Dutch ministries and their executive agencies'. *Public Management Review*, 13(6), 783–802.

Verhoest, K. (2005). 'Effects of autonomy, performance contracting, and competition on the performance of a public agency: A case study'. *Policy Studies Journal*, 33(2), 235–258.

Verhoest, K., Peters, B. G., Bouckaert, G., & Verschuere, B. (2004). 'The study of organisational autonomy: A conceptual review'. *Public Administration and Development*, 24(2), 101–118.

Voorn, B., Borst, R. T., & Blom, R. (2020). 'Business techniques as an explanation of the autonomy-performance link in corporatized entities: Evidence from Dutch municipally owned corporations'. *International Public Management Journal*, forthcoming. https://doi.org/10.1080/10967494.2020.1802632

West, W. F. (2005). 'Neutral competence and political responsiveness: An uneasy relationship'. *Policy Studies Journal*, 33(2), 147–160.

Wynen, J., Verhoest, K., Ongaro, E., Van Thiel, S., & in cooperation with the COBRA network. (2014). 'Innovation-oriented culture in the public sector: Do managerial autonomy and result control lead to innovation?'. *Public Management Review*, 16(1), 45–66.

Wynen, J., & Verhoest, K. (2015). 'Do NPM-type reforms lead to a cultural revolution within public sector organizations?'. *Public Management Review*, 17(3), 356–379.

Yesilkagit, K., & Van Thiel, S. (2008). 'Political influence and bureaucratic autonomy'. *Public Organization Review*, 8(2), 137–153.

4 Marketisation and public management

Although governments exist in large measure to fill the gaps left by imperfect markets, the state has always relied on privately owned organisations to perform both peripheral and core functions (Wettenhall 2005). The twentieth century expansion of the state into the large-scale provision of goods and services (from health and education to the so-called strategic industries) marked a break in trend rather than a continuation of one. Whether because of faltering growth, fiscal stress or an ideological change of tide, the waves of privatisation associated with the new public management have taken us back to the traditional blurry entwinement of business and government that had held sway for centuries before.

The increasing dependence on the private sector for the provision of public services provides the *raison d'etre* for an expanding industry of private sector organisations. The UK's National Audit Office (2016) reports that annual spending on contracts with the private and voluntary sectors now surpasses that spent on in-house provision. This means, by one measure at least, that UK publicly funded services are more likely to be provided by the private than the public sector. Waves of privatisation have eroded the presumption that some services or functions are, as Johnston and Girth (2012) put it, 'inherently governmental'. Indeed, the tables have turned to such a degree that the private sector is increasingly seen as the saviour of resource starved public services.

First and foremost then, marketisation is realised through traditional models of good procurement practice. The traditional contracting model sees the public sector advertise clearly specified functions to private sector suppliers whose bids are filtered through a competitive tendering process concluding in the offer of a contract to the organisation judged to promise best value. Markets – at least when managed through robust competitive tendering processes – have the virtue, so it is claimed, of disciplining government suppliers by making their contract contestable.

Frustrated by the limitations of traditional contracting, UK governments of the 1980s pioneered the large-scale transfer of public sector assets to private ownership. Formerly public sector services including the utilities, rail and post were privatised on the presumption that private sector resources – from investment funds to an entrepreneurialism – could unlock service improvement (Ramanadham 2019). More recently, the same sort of arguments have fuelled the creation of public–private hybrids (or partnerships) intended to renew formerly public sector asset like hospitals and schools.

Marketisation does not end with procurement of services from, or their transfer to, the private sector. Governments have also sought to simulate market conditions within the public sector by adopting policies which force organisations to compete for their funds. The first step in this marketisation process, as was discussed in the preceding chapter, requires the creation of relatively autonomous agencies with responsibility to ensure that they balance their books. The second step requires an institutional separation of the purchaser and provider of services such that the allocation of current funds is conditional in some way on the decisions of a similarly autonomous purchaser (Le Grand 1991). Schools and universities for example can be funded for each student they attract, or subject they study. Hospitals are funded per medical procedure, care homes by residents and so on. In a similar manner, investment funding can be allocated on the basis of grant competitions in which governments invest in organisations or places that submit the most attractive bid. Advocates of these practices suggest that organising services in this way serves to empower purchasers (whether governments or consumers) who can now walk away without the need for further explanation.

Quasi-markets of this form can be further buttressed through the introduction of a range of performance indicators which allow for comparison or 'yardstick competition' between alternative providers (whether they be schools, universities, hospitals or even police forces). Performance can be measured in this way through a range of process indicators (like inputs, outputs and outcomes) but also through simplified regulatory judgements. Detached from greater bureaucratic and professional allegiances, managerial careers now wax or wane on the back of their organisation's reputation as signified through performance league tables or regulatory judgements. Although not a proper market, public managers find themselves competing in market-like conditions deliberately established and maintained by public policy.

Reforms of this type have been introduced across the world in a bid to capture the merits of market forms of organisation. Economists tell us that, at their best, markets can minimise the unit costs of production (so-called technical efficiency) and allocate resources to the most efficient or satisfying applications (allocative efficiency). The latter, in particular, depends upon a series of processes from understanding the preferences of consumers to the state of the art in production and delivery. The motivation to stay close to customers and on top of technology is provided by a competitive fight for self-interest which serves to coordinate the interests of buyers and sellers as if, according to Adam Smith, by an 'invisible hand'. Governments have found it difficult to replicate the self-organising systems described by Smith. The incomplete processes of marketisation associated with the new public management have only managed to capture some of the efficiency benefits rehearsed by economists. This chapter considers the main forms of marketisation adopted by governments and the rather patchy way in which they have delivered only some of the benefits of free markets some of the time.

Contracting

The case for competitive contracting stands on the theoretical foundations of principal-agent theory. Focused on the design of contract and incentive systems to ensure an agent's compliance, the theory suggests that contracting will maximise value for money when exact specifications can be drawn up, outputs easily measured and inadequate suppliers quickly replaced (Donahue 1989, p. 45). The theory informs both national and international notions of good procurement practice while departures from it are often interpreted as evidence of incompetent or perhaps even corrupt government (National Audit Office 2020).

First used for peripheral goods and services with vibrant private sector markets, by the 1980s governments started to extend market testing to functions which had traditionally been provided by the state. By exposing hitherto protected (or monopoly) government services to competitive pressures, contracting promised, first and foremost, to reduce the costs of service delivery. In such a way, contracting emphasises the benefits likely to accrue from the process of competition rather than transfer of ownerships to the private sector. Caves and Christensen (1980, p. 974) explain that 'the oft noted inefficiency of government enterprises stems from their isolation from effective competition rather than their public ownership per se'.

Two reviews of the evidence suggest that contracting might work. Hodge concludes that 'the weight of evidence appears to support the notion that, on average, the unit cost of services is reduced through competitive tendering of public services' (Hodge 1998, p. 98). Although raising serious questions about the research methods adopted in many of the studies (with regard to the control of quality and transaction costs), Boyne (1998, p. 482) too acknowledges that on the face of it half of the empirical studies he reviewed reported contracting to be associated with 'lower spending and higher efficiency'. Both Hodge (1998) and Boyne (1998) are clear, however, that efficiency savings are far from guaranteed.

Differences in the contractibility of services go some way towards explaining the mixed results uncovered by empirical studies. Hefetz and Warner (2012) find that while tangible services delivered at scale delivered some successes, the extension of contracting to intangible services in rural areas produced more equivocal results. Theorists recognised – particularly in some of the softer, more intangible, aspects of service delivery – that it is impossible to write or police a complete contract (Hart 2003). As Domberger (1998, pp. 207–208) explains, the 'non-contractibility of quality' means that: 'In some circumstances it is not possible to specify formally the full range of service characteristics, which makes monitoring and enforcing contracts particularly difficult'.

Coase (1937) and then Williamson (1981) had warned that the costs of contracting in circumstances such as these may be so prohibitive as to make in-house provision a lower cost option than outsourcing through contracts. More specifically they explain that contracting is made more difficult (and in turn more expensive) by transaction costs attributable to complexity, uncertainty, infrequency, specificity, tangibility and interconnectedness of the product or service to be procured (Marsh 1998). Insuring against or else resolving problems attributable to these difficulties adds to the administrative costs of contracting. Girth et al. (2012, p. 888) suggest that by some estimates these transaction costs can add up to one quarter of the cost of the contract.

Aside from factors identified by principal agent theory and transaction costs, researchers also point to the importance of the contestability of supply markets. Contestability is realised most clearly when rigorous procurement processes are combined with competitive markets (Domberger & Jensen 1997). Where competitive markets make contractors conscious of their vulnerability they will focus on their core performance – improving the quality of the work and reducing the costs wherever possible – for fear that a failure to please their clients will lead to a loss of business (Bel et al. 2010). In this vein, it can be argued that it does not matter whether contracts are awarded to private, public or third sector suppliers since it is the process of competitive tendering and the state of contestability which provides the drive for increased efficiency (Hodge 1998).

Although contestability might be strongest in those services subject to regular and specific contracting, there is, as Johnston and Girth (2012, p. 7) put it, 'no clear consensus on an optimal number of bidders'. While on the one hand, a perfectly competitive market would, according to economists, require numerous buyers and sellers of a homogeneous product and freedom of entry and exit, Baumol and Willig (1986) argue that a fear that markets can be contested by rivals is sufficient. Cohen and Eimicke (2008, p. 104) report that the Mayor of Indianapolis Steve Goldsmith required a 'yellow pages test' of five or more listed companies before proceeding with competition or outsourcing. Both the theory of imperfect markets and some empirical evidence suggest, however, that far from ensuring contestability, a small number of suppliers operating in a local market provide more of an opportunity for collusion than contestability (Entwistle 2005).

Much empirical work suggests, however, that many of the markets facing governments are not fiercely contested. In a study of UK local government contracts advertised between 1989 and 1992, Walsh and Davies (1993, p. 67) found an average of just under one external bid per contest. Looking this time at US local government procurement decisions, Hefetz and Warner (2012, p. 299) find 'for many services there is not a competitive local market of alternative providers' and that competition (or more specifically the lack of it) was 'the most important characteristic determining sourcing choice' (Hefetz & Warner 2012, p. 303). Still in the US, Girth et al. (2012, p. 896) report that 'most of the 67 services analyzed are characterized by monopolistic or non-competitive markets'. Johnston and Girth (2012, p. 21) go on to document the 'significant levels of administrative resources are devoted to managing the market by creating, stimulating, and maintaining competition' (Johnston & Girth 2012, p. 21). 'Provider competition', they conclude, 'can be difficult to achieve and costly to sustain'.

Alongside the problem of specifying intangible service standards and ensuring contestable supply markets, the contracting model seems ill suited to the improvement of service quality. Quite the reverse, as Broms et al. (2020) explain, there are good theoretical reasons to think that competition will not only drive down prices but service quality as well. Bearing this out, evidence from Swedish residential care confirms

> that competition for the market does surprisingly little for quality: private entrepreneurs perform neither better nor worse under stiff competition, quality of care is approximately the same in those

public nursing homes that are exposed to the market as in those that are not.

(Broms et al. 2020, p. 540)

Empirical work has then come full circle. From pointing to the low hanging fruit of reduced contract prices that could be captured by competitive contracting, contemporary studies point to the limitations of the contracting model and the merits of returning services in-house through a process of reverse contracting (Hefetz & Warner 2004). Surveying the UK government's enthusiasm for the outsourcing of IT contracts, Cordella and Willcocks (2010, p. 87) conclude that contracting has led to 'the denigration of bureaucratic structures and values, despite the fact that bureaucracies in specific concrete forms can be the rich repository for values, skills, efficiency and effectiveness'.

Privatisation and partnership

The wholesale privatisation of government functions appeals to a different logic. Whereas the preceding section considered using the competitiveness of the market and the detail of the contract to maintain the power of the public sector principal, privatisation transfers that very principalship. In such a way, and in theory at least, the challenge (or risk) of providing formerly public services (like energy, water, waste and so forth) becomes the responsibility of private organisations.

Alongside a complete transfer of ownership, governments increasingly negotiate hybrid arrangements – often described as public–private partnerships – which are based on mixed ownership and a high level of trust (Bajari et al. 2009). As well as the transfer of risk and the injection of private sector resources, partnership promises a saving in the transaction costs of coordination. Processes of drawing up specifications, inviting competitive tenders and supervising contracts add considerably to the costs of contracting. By replacing these supervisory arrangements with longer contract periods, looser specifications and open book accounting, public–private partnerships promise to use trust to unlock resources that can improve performance. It is this prospectus that has fundamentally changed procurement practice in both the public and private sectors (Parker & Hartley 2003; Entwistle & Martin 2005). Whether these partnerships or 'long term infrastructure contracts', as Hodge and Greve (2009, p. 33) sensibly describe them, deliver the improvements they promise is hotly debated.

The advocates of wholesale privatisation and hybrid forms of public–private partnership argue, in simple terms, that the private sector has a performance advantage over the public sector. This case stands not on the competitiveness of the industry (which in many cases are dominated by just a few suppliers) but on claims of sectoral difference (Cohen & Eimicke 2008). Property rights theories suggest that the difference in the form of ownership between the public and private sector translate into important differences between the structure and behaviour of public and private sector organisations. Caves and Christensen (1980, p. 959) explain that because public ownership 'is diffused among all members of society' there is 'little economic incentive for any owner to monitor the behaviour of the firm's management'. In the private sector, by contrast – with much smaller numbers of owners and assets that are easily valued and exchanged – there is 'a much larger interest in knowing and controlling costs' (Christoffersen et al. 2007, p. 312).

These differences in ownership are likely to translate into divergent attitudes to the search for value. As the economists express it, the private sector is more attuned to the opportunity costs of the resources used in service delivery. More broadly, commentators describe the different basis of ownership as fostering a private sector culture which is more enterprising, flexible, innovative and less risk averse than its public counterpart (Donahue & Zeckhauser 2012; Osborne & Gaebler 1992). Van Ham and Koppenjan (2001, p. 597) explain that 'the involvement of private parties is desirable because on the one hand they operate more efficiently than public organizations but also because they possess the market experience and innovative creativity which public parties often lack'. More focused on outcomes than formal decision-making procedures and administrative oversight, private sector organisations can be less hampered by bureaucratic rules and controls (Rainey 1989).

One particular aspect of red tape seems particularly important. Whereas the borrowing of public sector agencies is determined by heavily contested political priorities, access to global finance allows private sector organisations to borrow in proportion to the surety and scale of their projected revenue stream albeit at higher cost than the state (Lonsdale 2005). This sectoral difference alone was at the heart of the UK's private finance initiative which has seen more than £60 billion of investment in schools, hospitals and transport infrastructure transferred to the private sector (National Audit Office 2018). Governments claimed that private sector finance (together with its keener eye for value and a better record of project delivery) allowed the refurbishment of assets (schools, hospitals, transport and energy infrastructure) which had for decades been starved of investment by political limits to borrowing.

Alongside better access to finance capital, private sector organisations can access a range of other scale economies because they offer more specialised services across government jurisdictions, and, increasingly, national boundaries. Research by Christoffersen et al. (2007, p. 312) finds that significant differences in the cost of public and private cleaning 'arises from differences in the ability to exploit economies of scale'. They go on to explain that the public sector is not well placed to capture these benefits partly because public managers are more focused on pleasing their bureaucratic stakeholders than hunting out the efficiency savings associated with increased scale (Christoffersen et al. 2007). But even with the requisite motivation, public managers may struggle to find scale simply because their jurisdictions are so small. Pérez-López et al. (2016, p. 591) describe scale as key to the efficiency of waste collection services but beyond the reach of small municipalities. While in theory – as is considered in the next chapter – small jurisdictions could be combined through shared services or public–public partnership, the conflicting accountability arrangements of statutory organisations can make this difficult.

While the theory is attractive, the empirical evidence tells a more equivocal story. Some studies do indeed point to private sector superiority. On the basis of a study of oil companies in the public and private sectors, Wolf finds results 'supportive of the hypothesis that "ownership matters" in the sense that private ownership encourages better performance and greater efficiency than state ownership does' (Wolf 2009, p. 2650). Boitani et al. (2013) suggest that these ownership advantages can be captured through partnership although they note that the productivity of mixed ownership firms – hybrid or partnership-type arrangements – is determined by the degree of private ownership.

Bel et al. (2010) come to more sceptical conclusions. Based on a meta-analysis of the privatisation of water and waste services, Bel et al. (2010) 'do not find a genuine empirical effect of cost savings resulting from private production'. Indeed, they suggest that the efficiency savings they do find are more attributable to processes of competition than the ownership of assets. Other work – this time in areas with more intangible services – comes to similar conclusions. In a study of regulatory judgements of private, public and non-profit care homes, Barron and West (2017, p. 137) find that: 'Controlling for a range of facility characteristics such as age and size' the private homes had lower quality ratings 'over a range of 20 measures, including safety, effectiveness, respect, meeting needs and leadership'. Based on a study of English local governments, Andrews and Entwistle (2015, p. 273) suggest that only those governments with a lavishly financed client capacity 'are able to realise productive efficiency gains from public private partnership'.

Hodge and Greve (2017) make the point that in contrast to the contracting arrangements of the past – which were justified purely on grounds of value for money – public–private partnerships promise to unlock a much wider spectrum of performance improvements. Judged on value for money alone, Hodge and Greve (2009) find something of an even balance between studies supporting and questioning the efficiency savings of public–private partnerships. They make the point that, precisely because these arrangements extend over decades, a final judgement about their value for money must wait. The transfer of risk – which has particular importance in the calculation of value for money (Ball et al. 2003) – can only be properly evaluated at the conclusion of the project when the risks have run their course. Politically, however, the public–private partnership approach to infrastructure development has proved attractive enough to be exported around the world and consistently supported by UK governments of different political persuasions for nearly three decades.

Quasi-markets

While contracting and privatisation expose public functions to real albeit imperfect markets, not everything can be marketised in this way. In cases where governments are reluctant to privatise either the principal or agent roles, they can simulate some aspects of marketisation by the introduction of purchaser-provider splits. Whereas the funding decisions 'of politicians, bureaucrats and professionals operating in a bureaucratic environment' (Le Grand 1991, p. 1256) all too often proved 'unresponsive to the needs and wants of the very people it was set up to help', quasi-market reforms promise to empower the public service consumer. When 'confronted with the uncooperative teacher, with the insensitive consultant, or with the recalcitrant housing clerk' quasi-market reforms would give service users – particularly those without the resources to seek private sector solutions – the power to 'take their business elsewhere' (Le Grand 1991, pp. 1262–1263).

More focused on allocative than technical efficiency, quasi-market reforms are not particularly suited to containing or reducing cost. Indeed, Le Grand (1991) cites a series of good reasons – from set up and marketing to competition for inputs – to think that quasi-market reforms may actually increase the costs of provision. In education for example, allocative efficiency should be improved, in theory at least, by the schools' freedom 'to make choices specifically adapted to their respective situations and to differentiate their provision from that of competing schools' (Dumay & Dupriez 2014, p. 511). Although central to the appeal of quasi-market reforms, improvements in allocative efficiency promised by increased consumer choice have proved difficult to unlock. The problem as anticipated by Le Grand (1991) is that in most cases a lack of redundancy in public sector capacity means that newly empowered purchasers can only spend their money at the only hospital or school operating in their local area. Without reform, imperfections in the supply side might have the perverse effect of empowering monopoly providers to cherry pick the most attractive clients, leading to a concentration of 'bad risks' and potentially stretched services 'among the poorer and deprived' (Le Grand 1991, p. 1266). Eyeing quasi-market reforms in education, Glennerster (1991, p. 1271) reasons that 'other things being equal' an internal market will produce 'a selective system of education'. Since, as he puts it, 'Any school entrepreneur acting rationally would seek to exclude pupils who would drag down their overall performance' (Glennerster 1991, p. 1271).

Some empirical analysis of the outcomes of quasi-market reforms bears out these predictions. Dumay and Dupriez's (2014, p. 510) analysis of PISA data suggests that quasi-market reforms tend 'to be associated with a stronger link between schools' social composition and student achievement'. In a bid to address the monopoly power of local schools, governments in both the UK and the US have legislated to allow the introduction of free or charter schools irrespective of a traditional analysis of local need. Analysis of the composition of free schools in the UK suggests, however, that despite their location in areas of above average deprivation, the new schools recruit a student body which is 'more affluent' than the neighbourhood of the school (Allen & Higham 2018, p. 191). They go on to conclude that the introduction of free schools tended to 'reproduce socio-economic inequalities through social selection' (Allen & Higham 2018, p. 211).

Other work, however, suggests that fears of cream skimming have been exaggerated. Jilke et al.'s (2018) study of the way in which Flemish care homes responded to information requests from minority and non-minority sounding names suggested no evidence of cream skimming among public sector facilities. Although it has to be said that their exoneration does not extend to the private sector organisations in their sample. Other studies suggest that when efforts are made to provide purchasers with meaningful choice, quasi-markets can have positive effects. Scholars working in this area suggest that increased choice can be tied to improvements in quality of provision and the satisfaction of service users. Gaynor et al. (2013, p. 163) report 'strong evidence' that quasi-market reforms introduced into the UK's NHS – with fixed prices and guaranteed choice – sparked a competitive search for improvements in quality which 'resulted in significant improvements in mortality and reductions in length-of-stay without changes in total expenditure or increases in expenditure per patient'. Bergman et al. (2018, p. 15) also find that 'freedom of choice and freedom of entry' introduced into Swedish tax-financed homecare generated 'higher user satisfaction without significantly increasing costs'.

With real fees, real debt and much more competition than could ever be possible at school level, higher education has provided one of the most advanced experiments in the construction of quasi-markets. Even here, however, commentators have been quick to identify many of the features associated with market failure (Marginson 2013). Problems stem, according to Dill (1997), from the absence of reliable measures of the added value of a university education. Without a proper measure of the value of a degree, students and employers make choices on the basis of university status which are strongly tied to the more measurable dimension of research performance. But even if reliable measures of value could be established, it is not clear that marketisation would be a success. Molesworth et al. (2009) argue that by turning students into consumers of vocational products, marketisation changes the very purposes of higher education. They write that processes of marketisation have changed the core role of higher education from the critique of dominant norms to socialisation into them (Molesworth et al. 2009; Naidoo & Jamieson 2005). Empirical work bears this out. Based on a study of changes in applications and admissions coincident with the tripling of university fees in England, Sá (2019) finds a new preference for vocational courses promising better pay and prospects. He writes that 'faced with higher fees and a higher level of debt, students choose courses that offer better employment prospects and allow them to pay off debt more quickly after graduation' (Sá 2019, p. 631).

The quasi-market model has also been used as a way of distributing funds to local governments or other agencies. Whereas bureaucracy allocates resources through a centrally designed need-based formula of some sort, the market model requires would be recipients to enter a bidding contest for investment funds (Benz 2007). In regeneration, for example (Hutchinson 1997), bidders may point either to the scale of their problems or else the promise of their potential (in so-called ugly and beauty contests). John et al. (2004, p. 406) explain that in theory at least 'bidders make promises to improve public services in order to get ahead of their rivals' while in picking the best bids 'sponsors maximize social welfare'. In a study of the allocation of regeneration funds amongst English local governments, John et al. (2004, 405) find, however, that 'successive rounds did not greatly improve the quality of the bids' nor did they 'systematically reward needy communities' but they did show a tendency to divert resources to ministers own constituencies and to waste resources of unsuccessful bidders 'for no obvious advantages' (John et al. 2004, p. 424). Based on a case study of a winning city's attempts to deliver the plans promised in a competition for cycling infrastructure development, White et al. (2020, p. 173) conclude that 'competitive funding is likely to encourage authorities to present bids that are largely detached from the realities of implementing infrastructure, thus leading to difficulties once funding has been awarded'.

Yardstick competition

The effectiveness of quasi-market reforms depends in no small measure on the information made available to prospective purchasers. Accordingly, governments have increasingly required service providers to generate a panoply of performance information at the same time as they have encouraged regulators to publish simplified judgements of service and management quality. In theory, information of this sort, particularly when represented in user-friendly league tables, should help service users make choices between alternative providers. Whether of course they are the right choices is debatable. Leckie and Goldstein (2011) make the point that past performance – particularly in the case of long-term decisions like school choice – may not provide a good basis for predicting the future. Reliable or not, work by Gibbons et al. (2015, p. 148) on the UK's higher education quasi-market finds student satisfaction scores as represented in high-profile university league tables 'have a small statistically significant effect on applications at the university-subject level'.

The efficacy of performance information does not, however, depend exclusively on the opportunity for public service users to choose between different providers. The theory of 'yardstick competition' suggests that voters, politicians, managers and other stakeholders may also use this information to make relative judgements about the performance of public service providers. Yardstick competition was first used as a way of controlling prices in regulated industries. The theory suggests that in the absence of a proper market, regulators can force organisations to compete (on cost or other measures of performance) with the 'shadows' of comparable organisations (Shleifer 1985).

Salmon (1987) applies this logic to competition between local governments. Bracketing off Tiebout style relocation, governments that do not compete for custom may still compete for reputation or rank. In such a way, local government performance relative to comparable organisations might be used by voters to decide whether or not they will support the incumbent administration. Bearing this out, James and John (2007, p. 574) find that poorly graded local services lead to a '6% loss of support' for the incumbent party. As Boyne et al. (2009, p. 1282) explain, 'the opposition becomes relatively more attractive when local governments have low performance' but that, unjustly perhaps, 'incumbent administrations do not get a reward for achieving high performance'. Managers too are affected by yardstick comparisons. Boyne et al. (2010, p. i276) find that 'Central government's perceptions of performance, and to some extent also local citizens' satisfaction with services, predict the rate of senior management turnover in English local governments'.

Yardsticks are not only used by citizens to judge the performance of incumbents. Politicians too may use them to inform their strategy. Eyeing their position in the polls some politicians may, as Besley and Case (1995, p. 26) put it, seek to 'trim tax rate increases which put them out of line with their neighbors'. Ferraresi's (2020) empirical analysis of the spending decisions of neighbouring Italian municipalities lends support to the yardstick hypothesis particularly when political control is contested. Managers also may benchmark with the best organisations in the field as denoted by league tables or award schemes, purposively imitating the characteristics of their more successful competitors (Ashworth et al. 2009). In such a way, yardsticks do more than provide a digestible account of relative performance for external stakeholders, they are used as tools by managers to prompt and direct change programmes. Commenting on league tables used in the UK's NHS, Adab et al. (2002, p. 96) explain that in theory at least publication should stimulate 'competition, and that, as each provider adopts "best practice", the quality of services will improve'. This competition will in the long run, according to Benz (2012, p. 254), induce 'mutual adjustment, learning and qualitative improvement of performance'.

It is not guaranteed, however, that benchmarking information will be used in this way. Benz (2012) argues that learning depends upon the perception of the yardsticks, the working of incentives, organisational capacity and agreement over goals and standards. Based on a study of performance management in North Carolina, Ammons and Rivenbark (2008) distinguish between three different responses to yardstick comparisons. 'Reluctant comparers' rejected the legitimacy of external comparison, preferring instead to look at historical benchmarks. The cautious comparers would countenance comparison only with 'a select set of cities generally considered to be of a like nature by community leaders or citizens in general' (Ammons & Rivenbark 2008, p. 311). Only the last (and small) group of 'enthusiastic comparers' were prepared to 'embrace comparisons even when the initial results of these comparisons reveal their own performance to be disappointing' (Ammons & Rivenbark 2008, p. 313). Moynihan and Pandey (2010, p. 861) explain that the positive effects of performance comparison require 'not just a supply-side approach that ensures that useful information is easily available but also a demand-side approach that fosters norms consistent with information use'.

The UK labour government's huge experiment in yardstick-type reforms – running through the first decade of the twenty-first century – addressed both the supply and demand side of the equation. Dubbed the modernisation agenda, a batch of policies – performance information, simplified regulatory judgements and even special awards for the best and the brightest – encouraged, and at times cajoled, UK local governments to compare themselves against, and in turn adopt the practices of, high-performing organisations (Downe & Martin 2006). Both qualitative (Entwistle 2011; Döring 2015) and quantitative (Ashworth et al. 2009) studies provide some evidence that local governments did what they were told. Although Ward and John's (2013, p. 22) analysis of the diffusion of good practice points to a preference for learning from geographically and politically proximate organisations, the Labour government's experiment had, albeit at considerable cost, established that yardstick competition does indeed encourage diffusion.

But still, the improvement effect of yardstick competition presumes that the real determinants of performance are both observable and transferable (Entwistle & Downe 2005). In place of the transfer of real improvements, new institutional theory suggests that yardstick competition may prompt the diffusion of fashionable – but not necessarily effective – reforms through organisational mimicry (Piazza & Abrahamson 2020). More concerned with their organisational reputation than long-term determinants of organisational performance, managers may have good reason to engage with performance yardsticks in symbolic ways (Doering et al. 2019). Gerrish and Spreen (2017) ask whether the introduction of financial yardsticks in North Carolina fostered a drive to real improvement or mere isomorphism as local government sought safety in average performance. They find that after 'the introduction of the benchmarking tool, North Carolina's local governments tended more closely toward isomorphism rather than improvement as they converged toward the group mean across several indicators' (Gerrish & Spree 2017, p. 613).

Conclusion

Marketisation has assumed a central place in contemporary public management. The evidence suggests, however, that these reforms are effective only in very specific ways and that they sometimes come with significant disadvantages. Contracting can reduce the costs of service provision although it is difficult to protect quality and, depending upon the service area, there may be weighty transaction costs. Privatisation in all of its guises can unlock new resources – from finance to project management – but it is sometimes associated with increased cost, diminished control but not the transfer of risk (National Audit Office 2018). Quasi-markets are associated with some improvements of service quality but again there are questions about whether those improvements are secured at the expense of more vulnerable groups. Finally, while there is some evidence that yardstick competition can foster the diffusion of new ideas, questions remain whether the improvement it delivers is more symbolic than real. In summary, marketisation certainly is not a panacea. It has proved difficult to transfer the full benefits of perfectly competitive markets – from consumer sovereignty to allocative efficiency – into the realm of public management.

Despite an underwhelming track record, it seems vanishingly unlikely that governments will ever dispense with the marketisation idea. The continuing enthusiasm for market forces in public management might then be explained by something other than efficiency. Ideological theories suggest that conservative or right-wing governments may simply have a preference for the private sector delivery of public services while left leaning governments prefer to deliver services in-house (Alonso & Andrews 2020). Alternatively, governments of both political persuasions may turn to markets as a way of disciplining powerful occupational groups (the professions and trade unions) which are empowered by bureaucratic and autonomous forms of organisation (Entwistle & Laffin 2005).

Alongside research into the efficiency and effectiveness of markets, public management scholars need to have regard to the political functions they fulfil. Marketisation might be regarded as politically successful even if its record on quality and efficiency is underwhelming.

References

Adab, P., Rouse, A. M., Mohammed, M. A., & Marshall, T. (2002). 'Performance league tables: The NHS deserves better'. *British Medical Journal*, 324(7329), 95–98.

Allen, R., & Higham, R. (2018). 'Quasi-markets, school diversity and social selection: Analysing the case of free schools in England, five years on'. *London Review of Education*, 16(2), 191–213.

Alonso, J. M., & Andrews, R. (2020). 'Political ideology and social services contracting: Evidence from a regression discontinuity design'. *Public Administration Review*, 80(5), 743–754.

Ammons, D. N., & Rivenbark, W. C. (2008). 'Factors influencing the use of performance data to improve municipal services: Evidence from the North Carolina benchmarking project'. *Public Administration Review*, 68(2), 304–318.

Andrews, R., & Entwistle, T. (2015). 'Public–private partnerships, management capacity and public service efficiency'. *Policy & Politics*, 43(2), 273–290.

Ashworth, R., Boyne, G., & Delbridge, R. (2009). 'Escape from the iron cage? Organizational change and isomorphic pressures in the public sector'. *Journal of Public Administration Research and Theory*, 19(1), 165–187.

Bajari, P., McMillan, R., & Tadelis, S. (2009). 'Auctions versus negotiations in procurement: An empirical analysis'. *Journal of Law, Economics, & Organization*, 25(2), 372–399.

Ball, R., Heafey, M., & King, D. (2003). 'Risk transfer and value for money in PFI projects'. *Public Management Review*, 5(2), 279–290.

Barron, D. N., & West, E. (2017). 'The quasi-market for adult residential care in the UK: Do for-profit, not-for-profit or public sector residential care and nursing homes provide better quality care?'. *Social Science & Medicine*, 179, 137–146.

Baumol, W. J., & Willig, R. D. (1986). 'Contestability: Developments since the book'. *Oxford Economic Papers*, 38(S), 9–36.

Bel, G., Fageda, X., & Warner, M. E. (2010). 'Is private production of public services cheaper than public production? A meta-regression analysis of solid waste and water services'. *Journal of Policy Analysis and Management*, 29(3), 553–577.

Benz, A. (2007). 'Inter-regional competition in co-operative federalism: New modes of multi-level governance in Germany'. *Regional and Federal Studies*, 17(4), 421–436.

Benz, A. (2012). 'Yardstick competition and policy learning in multi-level systems'. *Regional and Federal Studies*, 22(3), 251–267.

Bergman, M. A., Jordahl, H., & Lundberg, S. (2018). *Choice and Competition in the Welfare State: Home Care as the Ideal Quasi-Market* (No. 1213). Research Institute of Industrial Economics (IFN), Stockholm Working Paper.

Besley, T., & Case, A. (1995). 'Incumbent behavior: Vote-seeking, tax-setting, and yardstick competition'. *American Economic Review*, 85(1), 25–45.

Boitani, A., Nicolini, M., & Scarpa, C. (2013). 'Do competition and ownership matter? Evidence from local public transport in Europe'. *Applied Economics*, 45(11), 1419–1434.

Broms, R., Dahlström, C., & Nistotskaya, M. (2020). 'Competition and service quality: Evidence from Swedish residential care homes'. *Governance*, 33(3), 525–543.

Boyne, G.A. (1998). 'Bureaucratic theory meets reality: Public choice and service contracting in U.S. local government'. *Public Administration Review*, 58(6), 474–484.

Boyne, G. A., James, O., John, P., & Petrovsky, N. (2009). 'Democracy and government performance: Holding incumbents accountable in English local governments'. *The Journal of Politics*, 71(4), 1273–1284.

Boyne, G. A., James, O., John, P., & Petrovsky, N. (2010). 'Does public service performance affect top management turnover?'. *Journal of Public Administration Research and Theory*, 20(suppl 2), i261–i279.

Caves, D. W., & Christensen, L. R. (1980). 'The relative efficiency of public and private firms in a competitive environment: The case of Canadian railroads'. *Journal of Political Economy*, 88(5), 958–976.

Christoffersen, H., Paldam, M., & Würtz, A. H. (2007). 'Public versus private production and economies of scale'. *Public Choice*, 130(3), 311–328.

Coase, R. H. (1937). 'The nature of the firm'. *Economica*, 4(16), 386–405.

Cohen, S., & Eimicke, W. (2008). *The Responsible Contract Manager*. Washington, DC: Georgetown University Press.

Cordella, A., & Willcocks, L. (2010). 'Outsourcing, bureaucracy and public value'. *Government Information Quarterly*, 27(1), 82–88.

Dill, D. D. (1997). 'Higher education markets and public policy'. *Higher Education Policy*, 10(3-4), 167–185.

Doering, H., Downe, J., Elraz, H., & Martin, S. (2019). 'Organizational identity threats and aspirations in reputation management'. *Public Management Review*, 23(3), 376–396.

Domberger, S. (1998). *The Contracting Organization: A Strategic Guide to Outsourcing*. Oxford: Oxford University Press.

Domberger, S., & Jensen, P. (1997). 'Contracting out by the public sector: Theory, evidence, prospects'. *Oxford Review of Economic Policy*, 13(4), 67–78.

Donahue, J.D. (1989). *The Privatisation Decision: Public Ends, Private Means*. New York, NY: Basic Books.

Donahue, J. D., & Zeckhauser, R. J. (2012). *Collaborative Governance: Private Roles for Public Goals in Turbulent Times*. Princeton, NJ: Princeton University Press.

Döring, H., Downe, J., & Martin, S. (2015). 'Regulating public services: How public managers respond to external performance assessment'. *Public Administration Review*, 75(6), 867–877.

Downe, J., & Martin, S. (2006). 'Joined up policy in practice? The coherence and impacts of the local government modernisation agenda'. *Local Government Studies*, 32(4), 465–488.

Dumay, X., & Dupriez, V. (2014). 'Educational quasi-markets, school effectiveness and social inequalities'. *Journal of Education Policy*, 29(4), 510–531.

Entwistle, T. (2005). 'Why are local authorities reluctant to externalise (and do they have good reason)?'. *Environment and Planning C: Government and Policy*, 23(2), 191–206.

Entwistle, T. (2011). 'For appropriateness or consequences? Explaining organizational change in English local government'. *Public Administration*, 89(2), 661–680.

Entwistle, T., & Downe, J. (2005). 'Picking winners to define and disseminate best practice'. *Public Policy and Administration*, 20(4), 25–37.

Entwistle, T., & Laffin, M. (2005). 'A prehistory of the best value regime'. *Local Government Studies*, 31(2), 205–218.

Entwistle, T., & Martin, S. (2005). 'From competition to collaboration in public service delivery: A new agenda for research'. *Public Administration*, 83(1), 233–242.

Ferraresi, M. (2020). 'Political cycles, spatial interactions and yardstick competition: Evidence from Italian cities'. *Journal of Economic Geography*, 20(4), 1093–1115.

Gaynor, M., Moreno-Serra, R., & Propper, C. (2013). 'Death by market power: Reform, competition, and patient outcomes in the national health service'. *American Economic Journal: Economic Policy*, 5(4), 134–166.

Gerrish, E., & Spreen, T. L. (2017). 'Does benchmarking encourage improvement or convergence? Evaluating North Carolina's fiscal benchmarking tool'. *Journal of Public Administration Research and Theory*, 27(4), 596–614.

Gibbons, S., Neumayer, E., & Perkins, R. (2015). 'Student satisfaction, league tables and university applications: Evidence from Britain'. *Economics of Education Review*, 48, 148–164.

Girth, A. M., Hefetz, A., Johnston, J. M., & Warner, M. E. (2012). 'Outsourcing public service delivery: Management responses in noncompetitive markets'. *Public Administration Review*, 72(6), 887–900.

Glennerster, H. (1991). 'Quasi-markets for education?'. *The Economic Journal*, 101(408), 1268–1276.

Hart, O. (2003). 'Incomplete contracts and public ownership: Remarks, and an application to public–private partnerships'. *The Economic Journal*, 113(486), C69–C76.

Hefetz, A., & Warner, M. (2004). 'Privatization and its reverse: Explaining the dynamics of the government contracting process'. *Journal of Public Administration Research and Theory*, 14(2), 171–190.

Hefetz, A., & Warner, M. E. (2012). 'Contracting or public delivery? The importance of service, market, and management characteristics'. *Journal of Public Administration Research and Theory*, 22(2), 289–317.

Hodge, G. (1998). 'Contracting public services: A meta-analytic perspective of the international evidence'. *Australian Journal of Public Administration*, 57(4), 98–110.

Hodge, G. A., & Greve, C. (2009). 'Public private partnerships: The passage of time permits a sober reflection'. *Economic Affairs*, 29, 33–39.

Hodge, G. A., & Greve, C. (2017). 'On public–private partnership performance: A contemporary review'. *Public Works Management & Policy*, 22(1), 55–78.

Hutchinson, J. (1997). 'Regenerating the counties: The case of the single regeneration budget challenge fund'. *Local Economy*, 12(1), 38–54.

James, O., & John, P. (2007). 'Public management at the ballot box: Performance information and electoral support for incumbent English local governments'. *Journal of Public Administration Research and Theory*, 21(3), 399–418.

Jilke, S., Van Dooren, W., & Rys, S. (2018). 'Discrimination and administrative burden in public service markets: Does a public–private difference exist?'. *Journal of Public Administration Research and Theory*, 28(3), 423–439.

John, P., Ward, H., & Dowding, K. (2004). 'The bidding game: Competitive funding regimes and the political targeting of urban programme schemes'. *British Journal of Political Science*, 34(3), 405–428.

Johnston, J. M., & Girth, A. M. (2012). 'Government contracts and "managing the market" exploring the costs of strategic management responses to weak vendor competition'. *Administration & Society*, 44(1), 3–29.

Leckie, G., & Goldstein, H. (2011). 'A note on the limitations of school league tables to inform school choice'. *Journal of the Royal Statistical Society: Series A*, 174(3), 833–836.

Le Grand, J. (1991). 'Quasi-markets and social policy'. *The Economic Journal*, 101(408), 1256–1267.

Lonsdale, C. (2005). 'Post-contractual lock-in and the UK private finance initiative (PFI): The cases of National Savings and Investments and the Lord Chancellor's Department'. *Public Administration*, 83(1), 67–88.

Marginson, S. (2013). 'The impossibility of capitalist markets in higher education'. *Journal of Education Policy*, 28(3), 353–370.

Marsh, A. (1998). 'Local governance: The relevance of transaction cost economics'. *Local Government Studies*, 24(1), 1–18.

Molesworth, M., Nixon, E., & Scullion, R. (2009). 'Having, being and higher education: The marketisation of the university and the transformation of the student into consumer'. *Teaching in Higher Education*, 14(3), 277–287.

Moynihan, D. P., & Pandey, S. K. (2010). 'The big question for performance management: Why do managers use performance information?'. *Journal of Public Administration Research and Theory*, 20(4), 849–866.

Naidoo, R., & Jamieson, I. (2005). 'Empowering participants or corroding learning? Towards a research agenda on the impact of student consumerism in higher education'. *Journal of Education Policy*, 20(3), 267–281.

National Audit Office. (2016). *Government Commercial and Contracting: An Overview of the NAO's Work*. London: NAO.

National Audit Office. (2018). *PFI and PF2*. London: NAO.

National Audit Office. (2020). *Investigation into Government Procurement during the COVID-19 Pandemic*. London: NAO.

Osborne, D., & Gaebler, T. (1992). *Reinventing Government: How the Entrepreneurial Spirit is Transforming the Public Sector*. New York, NY: Plume.

Parker, D., & Hartley, K. (2003). 'Transaction costs, relational contracting and public private partnerships: A case study of UK defence'. *Journal of Purchasing and Supply Management*, 9(3), 97–108.

Pérez-López, G., Prior, D., Zafra-Gómez, J. L., & Plata-Díaz, A. M. (2016). 'Cost efficiency in municipal solid waste service delivery. Alternative management forms in relation to local population size'. *European Journal of Operational Research*, 255(2), 583–592.

Piazza, A., & Abrahamson, E. (2020). 'Fads and fashions in management practices: Taking stock and looking forward'. *International Journal of Management Reviews*, 22(3), 264–286.

Rainey, H. G. (1989). 'Public management: Recent research on the political context and managerial roles, structures, and behaviors'. *Journal of Management*, 15(2), 229–250.

Ramanadham, V. V. (Ed.). (2019). *Privatisation in the UK*. London: Routledge.

Sá, F. (2019). 'The effect of university fees on applications, attendance and course choice: Evidence from a natural experiment in the UK'. *Economica*, 86(343), 607–634.

Salmon, P. (1987). 'Decentralisation as an incentive scheme'. *Oxford Review of Economic Policy*, 3(2), 24–43.

Shleifer, A. (1985). 'A theory of yardstick competition'. *The RAND Journal of Economics*, 16(3), 319–327.

Van Ham, H., & Koppenjan, J. (2001). 'Building public-private partnerships: Assessing and managing risks in port development'. *Public Management Review*, 3(4), 593–616.

Walsh, K., & Davis, H. (1993). *Competition and Service: The Impact of the Local Government Act 1988*. London: HMSO.

Ward, H., & John, P. (2013). 'Competitive learning in yardstick competition: Testing models of policy diffusion with performance data'. *Political Science Research and Methods*, 1(1), 3.

Wettenhall, R. (2005). 'The public-private interface: Surveying the history'. In Hodge, G. & Greve, C. (Eds.), *The Challenge of Public-Private Partnerships: Learning from International Experience*, Cheltenham: Edward Elgar, 22–43.

White, C., Bloyce, D., & Thurston, M. (2020). 'The double-bind of competitive funding: Exploring the consequences of state-funded bidding processes in a locally managed cycling infrastructure project'. *European Journal of Transport and Infrastructure Research*, 20(4), 173–193.

Williamson, O. E. (1981). 'The economics of organization: The transaction cost approach'. *American Journal of Sociology*, 87(3), 548–577.

Wolf, C. (2009). 'Does ownership matter? The performance and efficiency of State Oil vs. Private Oil (1987–2006)'. *Energy Policy*, 37(7), 2642–2652.

5 Collaboration and public management

Collaborative approaches to public management promise to coordinate without the need for bureaucracy or markets. Networks or partnerships, as they are generally described, bring together a variety of organisations – embracing the public, private and voluntary sector – to work towards common goals galvanised by a spirit of good will (Dore 1983). Without the need for the rational legal authority of bureaucracy or the incentives of free markets, coordination is realised voluntarily through some degree of trust, equality and reciprocity. In theory at least collaboration promises new public governance's antidote to the disintegration of public services bequeathed by autonomy and market-type reforms of the new public management (Osborne 2006).

Collaborative governance is not though new. Governments have always relied on high trust relationships of various sorts to access and then coordinate resources held both within and beyond the state. Elazar (1964, p. 249) argues that cooperation between the US federal and state governments is as old as the constitution itself. Alongside intergovernmental relations, governments have long recognised the need for collaboration between the different sectors of society and economy (Macadam 1934). Corporatist arrangements for national planning embracing the peak representatives of industry and the trade unions appealed to, even if they did not realise, ideas of voluntary negotiation and agreement (Molina & Rhodes 2002; Wood 2000). At the level of the local state, urban regimes were built on the presumption that: 'Governing capacity is created and maintained by bringing together coalition partners with appropriate resources, nongovernmental as well as governmental' (Stone 1993, p. 1).

Although not new, the prominence, formality and transparency of partnership working is a relatively recent development as is the extension of the partnership approach to ever wider and more demanding areas of public policy. Collaborative approaches are now used to address a bewildering variety of different purposes. A number of scholars working in the field (Agranoff 2007; Keast et al. 2007) identify different degrees of collaborative activity ranging from simple information exchange in networks of relatively weak ties to the fully fledged joint delivery of services. The formalisation of partnerships tends to be commensurate with the increased intensity (and risk) of collaborative activity. Networks to facilitate information exchange require little in the way of governance, whereas the joint delivery of services often necessitates some degree of incorporation (Tompkinson 2007). Irrespective of the intent or scope of collaborative activity, the rise of the collaboration agenda is well explained by resource dependence and transaction cost theories.

Resource dependence theory captures the need for governments to leverage resources held across the public, private and community sectors. It is increasingly recognised that public sector agencies can no longer be treated as 'lonely organisations' (Hjern & Porter, 1981, p. 212). Wicked issues – like sustainability and youth unemployment – together with the increasingly important efficiency agenda, make it difficult for organisations operating within the traditional narrowly defined jurisdictions of the public sector to meet the challenges of the twenty-first century. Resources need to be combined if public expectations are to be met (Andrews & Entwistle 2010).

While resources can always be acquired through bureaucratic merger or large-scale contracts, transaction costs theory warns of the forbidding costs of these approaches. Mergers often disappoint because of the costs of reorganisation but also because of curvilinear long run cost curves which mean that 'no single size of government will be able to produce all services at the minimum possible cost' (Dollery & Fleming 2006, p. 274). Resources can of course be captured through free market transactions, but we have already seen how imperfect supply markets and intangible outputs ramp up the transaction costs of contracting. Recognising the deficiencies of bureaucratic integration and free market contracting, governments across the world look to partnerships as a lower cost form of coordination.

But the partnership/network agenda is not without its problems. First and foremost, it comes with its own transaction costs chalked up through the protracted negotiations necessary to get all of the partners on the same page (Dixon & Elston 2020). Even then, however, the decisions to emerge from those negotiations may owe more to the lowest common denominator and cognitive lock-in than formal rationality (Scharpf 1988; Hood 2000). Although fashionable, there can then be no guarantee that partnership will solve the problems put at its door or indeed that it will deliver outcome at lower cost than the traditional alternatives.

This chapter considers four ways in which collaborative governance – whether branded as cooperation, networks or partnerships – is used to address different problems facing the state. First, partnership is used as a way of managing the vertical relationships between higher and lower tiers of government. Recognising the need for negotiation between tiers, almost all multi-level systems have developed collaborative arrangements to negotiate the joint delivery of policies and programmes. Second, and perhaps most prominently, collaboration is used as a form of horizontal coordination to tackle the wicked issues that fall between local governments and other agencies working at the same level. Third, partnerships have been used specifically to share both back office and customer facing services in a bid to unlock economies of scale. Fourth and finally, partnerships are used as a way of engaging citizen-consumers in the co-production of policies and services.

These different types of partnership are grouped together because they depend primarily upon the cooperative mechanisms of trust, equality and reciprocity. This chapter does not include the new breed of public–private partnerships within its remit. These arrangements – established for the specific purpose of delivering large-scale infrastructure projects – rely to some significant degree on mechanisms of trust, but first and foremost they are contractual arrangements underwritten by market forces (Hodge & Greve 2010). Conversely, co-production-type arrangements are included here precisely because they depend on the cultivation and maintenance of trust. This chapter considers whether these collaborative arrangements are of the same categorical type, does good practice developed in one sphere of activity transfer to other spheres of collaborative activity. Does a particularly cooperative case of intergovernmental relations tell us something about how best to co-produce local services?

For multi-level governance

Although coined specifically to capture the complex patterns of governance across levels and sectors seen in the European Union, there are few states not fittingly described by the idea of multi-level governance. Hooghe and Marks (2003) identify two contrasting types. The first – or type I – suggests that each tier of government has the autonomy to pursue its programmes in its own relatively separate and clearly demarcated jurisdiction. The second – or type II – describes an intermingling of roles and responsibilities such that the same territory or policy domain is governed in some way by more than one and perhaps all tiers of government at the same time.

Type I fits the notion of layer cake federalism envisaged by the US and Canadian constitutions. Although a powerful idea which continues to influence constitutional designers and independence campaigners around the world (Entwistle et al. 2014), few commentators have ever regarded it as providing a reliable account of intergovernmental relations. Rather than focusing exclusively on the high politics of their jurisdiction, higher tier governments cannot help involving themselves in the low politics of service delivery (Bulpitt 1986). As early as 1933 Corwin (1933, p. 504) concluded that 'whatever validity dual federalism may once have had as a canon of constitutional construction it has since lost, both because of its logical irreconcilability with a host of modern decisions and because of its actual unworkability'.

Acknowledging the intermingling of powers and interdependence of state and federal government, US federalism is largely described more in terms of marble cake than layer cake, or more formally, Hooghe and Marks' type II of multi-level governance. There is consensus too in seeing that interdependence as having given rise to cooperative pattern of intergovernmental relations. Elazar (1964, p. 249) explains that cooperation emerged pretty much from independence such that 'virtually all the activities of government in the nineteenth century were shared activities, involving federal, state and local governments in their planning, financing and execution'. From the beginning, according to Watts (2006, p. 206) Canada too was 'characterized by intergovernmental interdependence'. Despite a strictly dualist constitution of 'watertight compartments', Canadian federalism still exhibits 'a rich practice of intergovernmental collaboration' (Gaudreault-DesBiens & Poirier 2017, p. 392).

The last twenty years of German federalism, by contrast is characterised by Kropp and Behnke (2016) as: 'Marble cake dreaming of layer cake'. In a period marked by concerted efforts to increase 'federal and Lander government's autonomy by decentralization and separating powers' (Benz & Sonnicksen 2018, p. 134) reformers have tried to take German federalism closer to the US ideal of dual federalism. But the reforms intended to disentangle the interlaced responsibilities of the marble cake had the unintended and contradictory effect of reinforcing cooperative federalism (Benz & Sonnicksen 2018). With 'more financial and responsibility entanglement than before' (Kropp & Behnke 2016, p. 668), German intergovernmental relations continues to be described in terms of 'intense cooperation and coordination as well as joint financing of tasks' (Kropp & Behnke 2016, p. 682).

Cooperative intergovernmental relations are not necessarily consensual. Elazar (1964) suggests that the cooperation word is used to describe a process of joint decision-making which emerges from complementary interests and resources. Relations between governments may still be 'fraught and antagonistic' (Phillimore & Fenna 2017) and on occasion perhaps more competitive or coercive than cooperative (Kincaid 1990). Watts (2006, p. 208) describes disputes as the essence of politics suggesting that the institutions of cooperative federalism are designed to manage the inevitable competition and conflict which result from governments working together. Watts (2006, p. 209) points to three institutions (or practices) as key to the management of these conflicts: informal interpersonal contacts, joint conferences or councils and intergovernmental agreements.

Agranoff's (2004) account of intergovernmental relations chimes with this analysis. He makes the important point that cooperative institutions of intergovernmental relations are key not only to successful policy delivery but also to the continued autonomy of sub-central governments. He describes a cooperative system of intergovernmental relations as characterised by: a commitment to power sharing; respect for the political opposition; acknowledgement of the separate development needs of the state and the regions; and a resolution not to treat sub-central governments as part of the central bureaucracy (Agranoff 2004).

It is perhaps for that reason that we see these institutional arrangements – or something like them – emerging in the most unlikely of places. In Spain, Börzel (2000, p. 41) describes processes of European integration as prompting the establishment of new cooperative and hitherto alien procedures which allowed Spain's autonomous communities 'to participate in the formulation and implementation of European policies'. The conflictual history of Spanish intergovernmental relations confirms that the shared competencies of cooperative federalism are not a guarantee of consensus. However, in a study of cases before Spain's constitutional court, Harguindéguy et al. (2021) suggest that sectoral conferences, cooperation agreements and party-political congruence all served to limit the growth of federal conflicts.

Australian federalism is characterised in terms of the rising trends of centralisation and cooperation. Creeping centralisation means: 'There is now almost no area of State government operations that is ever completely untouched by Commonwealth funding, laws, policies or intentions' (Phillimore & Fenna 2017, p. 600). But the federal government still needs a cooperative relationship with the states for constitutional but also practical reasons, since it has no interest in taking on service delivery roles traditionally performed by the states (Fawcett & Marsh 2017). In such a way, the intermingling of responsibilities and finance has driven the growth of intergovernmental agreements and some formalisation of intergovernmental councils even if they still operate under the shadow of hierarchy (Phillimore & Fenna 2017).

Despite an ongoing process of devolution to Scotland, Northern Ireland and Wales, UK intergovernmental relations stands as something of an outlier to these trends. As in Australia, Swenden and McEwen (2014) describe the intergovernmental relations of the UK as conducted in the shadow of hierarchy. Unlike Australia, however, relations are still relatively new in constitutional terms and galvanised more by a search for autonomy than effective cooperation. Eyeing strains in the *ad hoc* and predominantly bi-lateral institutions highlighted by Brexit and Covid-19, McEwen et al. (2020, p. 639) call for 'more cooperative and productive relationships'. Drawing on lessons from Belgium, Spain, Italy, Canada and Australia, McEwen et al. (2020) suggest the need for a clearer and more detailed set of core principles (as expressed in the memorandum of understanding); strengthening the joint ministerial committee as a decision-making and conflict resolution body and resolving the ambiguity in the representation of England and the UK in intergovernmental negotiations. 'Finding mechanisms to facilitate intergovernmental cooperation' is, according to McEwen (2017, p. 685), 'one of the biggest challenges in UK territorial politics'.

For wicked issues

Alongside the need to coordinate across different tiers of government, the wicked or cross-cutting issues first identified in the late twentieth century call for improvements in horizontal coordination. Ling (2002, p. 616) explains that a perception grew in the 1990s that 'important goals of public policy cannot be delivered through the separate activities of existing organisations'. Problems like sustainability, community safety and education are increasingly understood as requiring multi-agency responses. Global warming obviously so (Bauer & Steurer 2014) but we also appreciate that crime cannot be solved simply through policing (Cherney 2004) and educational improvement requires partnerships which extend beyond the school gate (Sheldon & Epstein 2005).

Peters (2017) argues that the wicked label has been overused and that problems such as these might be difficult or complex but they are not wicked (at least not in the original sense of the term (Rittel & Webber

1973)). The way in which practitioners and commentators have latched onto the 'wicked' tag does, however, attest to important changes in the way in which we frame social problems. But it also says something of the narrow remits of the traditional and bureaucratic approach to public management. Policy was made on the presumption that publicly produced outputs would solve discreet problems in very specific jurisdictions. It is the tendency to frame social problems more broadly and to see bureaucracy as ill-suited to their resolution that drives the interest in network or partnership forms of governance.

Ferlie et al. (2011, p. 322) put the idea of wicked issues at the heart of their study of eight care networks in the UK's NHS. Defending the wicked issues label, they describe the networks they studied as focused on changing deeply ingrained patterns of behaviour by combining the efforts of multiple service providers operating in a variety of sectors. Kalesnikaite and Neshkova's (2021) study of the way in which US municipalities collaborate in response to sea level change also uses the wicked label. They find that the severity of the threat from rising sea levels is correlated with the degree of collaboration and the sectoral diversity of partners. They reason that when confronted by 'uncharted waters, governments realize the need for collaborators who can bring unique solutions to problems' (Kalesnikaite & Neshkova 2021, p. 412).

Understanding these networks and the factors associated with their performance is pressing business for public management researchers. Consisting of a variety of public and sometimes private and voluntary sector organisations with a stake in a key social problem, researchers use the ideas of network effectiveness or partnership performance to unlock the ingredients of good governance. Although complex and rapidly expanding, the empirical evidence points, albeit tentatively, to the positive effects of partnership approaches (Provan & Milward 1995; Andrews & Entwistle 2010). The literature suggests, however, that performance is contingent upon the context, structure and behaviour of the partnership in question.

First and foremost, research suggests that the context or environment matters. Stability in particular is important. Provan and Lemaire (2012, p. 646) explain that 'Significant disruptions in the pattern of relationships among the core organizations are especially difficult to overcome'. Munificent environments are helpful too, both in terms of the resources in the immediate environment but also in the form of technical assistance, grants or performance management afforded by an external sponsor. While there is some evidence to suggest that a demanding regulatory environment is positively associated with performance (Selden et al. 2006), excessively bureaucratic or competitive environments may undermine the voluntarism at the heart of collaborative endeavours (Entwistle et al. 2007). As Choi and Moynihan (2019) explain efforts to tighten performance management within an agency serve to undercut capacity for collaborative approaches to performance management with external partners.

Second, the structure of the network in terms of the interactions between member organisations and the formality of collaborative processes seem important. Provan and Lemaire (2012, p. 643) explain that when contacts between organisations 'are built around a single representative in an organisation, they may be tenuous'. A multiplicity of ties, however, will prove 'stronger and more intensive' (Provan & Lemaire 2012, p. 642). Overall network effectiveness can be significantly enhanced when network goals and interests are understood and accepted through meaningful involvement by multiple members of organisations in the network. Formalisation refers to the rules of the network or partnership: the extent to which the processes of collaboration are codified through established procedures or written documents. Formalisation can extend to the organisation of meetings, agendas, minutes, service level agreements, strategies and performance management. When actors and other stakeholders are aware of 'the availability of information about decision-making moments', formalisation improves accountability which in turn, according to Turrini et al. (2010, p. 542), 'influences the commitment of member organisations' to the benefit of quality of output and the sustainability of the network.

Finally, networks need to be managed. They need, as Provan and Lemaire (2012, p. 644) put it, a 'network facilitator, intermediary, hub firm or weaver'. While there are debates about whether managing between organisations is different to managing within them, there is a reasonable consensus on the activities which are positively associated with improved performance. Commentators use different terms – Turrini et al. (2010) describe the tasks as networking, buffering and steering; Huxham and Vangen talk in terms of embracing, empowering and mobilising; McGuire (2002) prefers: activation, framing, mobilising and synthesising – but all, in essence, describe very similar managerial activities. Klijn et al. (2010, p. 1069) find that exploring and connecting strategies are the most important. Exploring involves clarifying the 'goals and perceptions of actors'. Connecting involves the network manager identifying 'the actors required for an initiative' and then persuading them to invest their resources. Like Vangen and Huxham's (2003, pp. 69–70) diagnosis of the need for 'collaborative thuggery' to deal with members of the partnership 'who are not on board', 'ill informed' or 'cannot mutually communicate', Klijn et al. (2010) talk of a need for managers to 'deactivate' actors whose contributions have become counterproductive. Klijn et al. (2010, p. 1077) conclude that 'management matters far more than organization'.

Although there is some consistency in the messages emerging from network effectiveness research, there is also a recognition that there is unlikely to be a one best form of governance. In their review of the literature, Cristofoli et al. (2017) highlight a number of studies which adopt a contingency approach to network effectiveness in recognising that the ingredients for improved performance may vary between different contexts or applications. In this manner, Siciliano et al.'s (2021) longitudinal study of the outcomes of network governance in Iowa suggests that while network centralisation and stability deliver reductions in crime, private sector partners are key to improvements in economic development.

For shared services

While public–public partnerships emerge for a number of different reasons (Dixon & Elston 2020), the shared service agenda assumed particular importance after the financial crisis of 2008 (Warner et al. 2020). Small public service organisations have been encouraged to share their services with their neighbours in a bid to increase efficiency through economies of scale (Elston & Dixon 2020). Inter-municipal cooperation is particularly attractive to those governments without the political inclination or practical opportunity to outsource to private providers (Hefetz & Warner 2012).

Scale economies are particularly associated with capital intensive services like waste and transport but any specific asset – like human capital – has the same potential, in theory at least, to promise decreasing average costs. The per unit service cost for small organisations to employ specifically trained professionals in law, human resources and procurement, for example, is likely to be higher than for those operating at greater scale. In such a way, we can add back office functions like human resource management, legal services and procurement to our list of services likely to benefit from a move towards shared services.

Empirical evidence is though mixed. Bel and Warner's (2015) review of the literature finds that much of the work is focused on the sharing of waste services between very small European local governments. But even this limited sample of studies suggests that the efficiency gains of sharing may be limited to the smallest of organisations. Based on a study of waste services in 771 Spanish municipalities, Pérez-López et al.'s (2016, p. 591) findings bear this out. They report that while shared services work well for smaller municipalities (with under 20,000 inhabitants), 'private operators obtain higher levels of efficiency' for larger populations. Bel and Sebő's (2021, p. 178) meta-analysis of service sharing (again predominantly in the field of waste) adds yet more weight to this conclusion. As they write, it is the 'municipalities with small population sizes' that tend to find inter-municipal cooperation the 'more cost advantageous' (Bel & Sebő 2021, p. 178).

Alongside population size, Aldag et al.'s (2020, p. 285) analysis of 20 years of service sharing in New York State suggests 'cost savings are heavily dependent on the characteristics of each service'. Consistent with their dependence on specific forms of capital, only five services – 'police, library, solid waste management, sewer, and roads and highways' – delivered cost savings (Aldag et al. 2020, p. 284). By contrast two service areas – elderly care and planning – suggest that sharing increases costs, albeit perhaps because these collaborations are focused on other dimensions of service improvement. Aldag et al.'s (2020) findings serve as a reminder that unit costs do not inevitably decline with increases in scale. Each service has different long run cost curves as Dollery and Fleming (2006, p. 274) explain, such that 'the most efficient level of production will depend on the type of service'. Increases in the scale of some services might translate more into diseconomies than economies.

Elston and Dixon's (2020) study of back office service sharing in 300 English local authorities bears this out. Although three quarters of their sample participated in at least one shared service, they found 'no significant relationship' between shared service collaboration and 'change in the proportion of resources spent on administration' (Elston & Dixon 2020, p. 123). They point to unrealistic presumptions about the homogeneity of local services and the extent of untapped scale economies. In particular, their findings suggest that away from the capital intensive services at the heart of Aldag et al.'s (2020) study, the professional and clerical services associated with back office functions are unlikely to benefit from increases in scale.

The disappointing results of empirical research might in part be explained by the varied ways in which services have been shared. Tomkinson (2007) identifies four models of governance. The intraservice model describes the sharing of part of a service through formal procurement or informal exchange. In the service model, one organisation transfers service delivery responsibility to another organisation managed through a service level agreement. Tomkinson's 'corporatist model' involves the creation of a joint board or committee to oversee the delivery of the shared service. Whereas the 'supra-corporate model', described by Tomkinson, involves two or more councils establishing a special purpose vehicle – a limited company or trust of some form – to deliver a specified service. The model gives the service provider greater autonomy (with all the attendant benefits) at the price of reduced control, and perhaps accountability, for the member authorities. Some of these models of governance (and others besides) may work better than others but as yet few studies have collected data at such a granular level. Bel and Sebő (2021) observe, however, that it was the studies of service sharing with supramunicipal governments in their meta-analysis that tended to find the most marked cost savings.

Boon (2018) too attributes some of the failed promise of shared service centres to the different ways in which relationships between commissioners and providers of services are managed. Services procured through principal agent contracting are according to Boon (2018) prone to all of the problems described in Chapter 4, but they are further complicated by the presence of plural principals. Shared service providers build scale by delivering services to multiple organisations in such a way as to create 'coordination issues between principals' which might make it difficult to steer the provider effectively (Boon 2018, p. 99). Boon argues that some of the problems of principal-agent relationships might be overcome by adopting a stewardship (or collaborative) approach to relationship management (Davis et al. 1997; Dollery et al. 2011). He calls for research 'to understand under what conditions stewardship governance models are more likely to lead to superior performance and collaboration, and how stewardship governance models can be designed' (Boon 2018, p. 103).

For co-production

Curiously, our understanding of perhaps the most important partnership – that between the producers and consumers of public services – is the least developed. Services by their very nature depend upon positive engagement between the producers and consumers (Osborne et al. 2013). School education depends upon a partnership between teachers and parents. Waste services depend upon our willingness to separate our recyclables and leave them on the pavement at the appropriate time. Changes in our behaviour – whether in education or waste recycling – require, according to Stoker (2006, p. 48), 'intensive dialogue and high levels of trust between the public and authorities'.

Recognising the intrinsic interdependence of consumers and producers in service delivery led Elinor Ostrom and colleagues to coin the term co-production, 'an emerging conception of the service delivery process', according to Brudney and England (1983, p. 59), 'which envisions direct citizen involvement in the design and delivery of city services with professional service agents'. Although central to the delivery of all public services and long recognised, academic interest in co-production has waxed and waned over time (Spoor 1939; Thomas 2013; Nabatchi 2017). While the promise of untapped resources might explain the heightening of interest in the decade or so since the financial crisis, co-production has also been put in the spotlight by the huge and growing interest in the idea of public value. Moore's (1995) reorientation of public services around the value they create for economy and society calls for much closer engagement between governments and citizens (Lindgreen et al. 2019). Rather than just seeing citizen engagement as normatively desirable, the linked ideas of public value and co-production underline the instrumental benefits as well. The World Health Organization, for example, 'expects co-production to improve access, responsiveness to community needs and customer satisfaction and result in a better relationship between individual care users and care providers' (cited in Jaspers & Steen 2019, p. 606).

Capitalising on the co-production idea has though proved difficult. Partly this is because of the varied approaches to the definition of the idea itself and the actors embraced by it. Given that the provision of all services requires some measure of interaction between producers and consumers (or subjects at its most minimal), it might be said that all services are co-produced. There is a danger then, as Nabatchi et al. (2017, p. 768) put it, that 'coproduction is used indiscriminately to describe virtually any activity involving people other than government'. The reverse also holds true, in that lots of activities akin to co-production are labelled in different ways. Other disciplines use terms like participatory budgeting and stakeholder or citizen engagement to address very similar ideas (de Sousa Santos 1998; Noland & Phillips 2010; Gaventa & Barrett 2012). While explaining something of its popularity, the fuzzy definition and application of the term makes co-production vulnerable to Wildavsky's (1973) quip about planning that if it is 'everything, maybe it's nothing'.

In a bid to inject some terminological clarity, Nabatchi et al. (2017, p. 769) suggest that co-production should be defined broadly 'as an umbrella term that captures a wide variety of activities that can occur in any phase of the public service cycle and in which state and lay actors work together to produce benefits'. They further propose that co-production can occur at three different levels (individual, group and community) and that it can feed into four different stages of the service cycle (commissioning, design, delivery and assessment). Any evaluation of the benefits of co-production would need to acknowledge the multi-dimensional aspects as perceived by different stakeholders.

There is some evidence that public participation can contribute to performance improvement. Neshkova and Guo's (2012, p. 285) study of participation in US state transport agencies leads them to conclude 'that public agencies can become more efficient and effective by opening their decision-making processes to the public and taking advantage of the contextual knowledge and practical advice it has to offer'. More recently, in a study of the co-production of environmental services like clogged drains, broken streetlights and damaged roads in Jakarta, Allen et al. (2020, p. 6) find an 'increase in e-participation, in a form of providing service feedback, is positively related to better service performance'.

So, if co-production adds value, how can governments encourage citizens to do more of it? The good news is that there seems to be something of an untapped reservoir of willingness amongst citizens to do more. More than 70% of James and Jilke's (2020) sample of US survey respondents claimed a willingness to co-produce. Alford and Yates (2016) suggest that acknowledging the reciprocal relationship between governments and citizens is key to unlocking this resource. First, they suggest that government should recognise that co-producers like to work alone without the need to engage with other citizens or government officials. Second, that governments should try to provide some private value since co-producers are not entirely motivated by altruism. Third, governments should make both the theory and practice of citizen work as straightforward as possible.

All of these require some sort of investment, as Bovaird and Loeffler (2012, p. 1119) snappily put it: 'Co-production may be value for money, but it usually cannot produce value without money'. The investment should not, however, take the form of an explicit payment. Voorberg et al.'s (2018) experiments provide some support for the idea that extrinsic rewards may crowd out intrinsic motivation. They suggest that low-level incentives to aid the integration of refugees did not increase citizen willingness to co-produce and that a substantial increase in the incentive prompted only a slight increase in willingness. They conclude that 'financial incentives are not a very cost-efficient instrument to stimulate coproduction' (Voorberg et al. 2018, p. 864). Further evidence of the fragility of intrinsic motivation comes from James and Jilke's (2020) analysis of the relationship between co-production and marketisation. Their experiments suggest that the private sector delivery of public services decreased both the 'probability of volunteering' and 'the amount of time participants were willing to contribute' to co-production (James & Jilke 2020, p. 953).

Finally, we need to remember that co-production, in common with all of the forms of coordination considered in this book, comes at a cost and with the potential to dysfunction. A rapidly expanding literature points to the dark side of co-production in the form of a series of unintended or in some cases perhaps intended consequences. Alongside the need for investment both to facilitate communication and implement changes to emerge from it, Steen et al. (2018) point to three problems. First, they suggest that governments may deliberately embrace co-production in a bid to dodge or at least blur responsibility or accountability for a particular problem or service. Second, although intended to empower, co-production might accentuate the advantages enjoyed by the relatively privileged who may find it easier to communicate their priorities over others. Third and finally, the direct democracy of co-production may deprive representative institutions, and those who participate in them, of choice opportunities they used to enjoy.

Conclusion

This chapter has reviewed collaborative approaches to coordination in intergovernmental relations, wicked issues, shared services and co-production. From public management's functional perspective, these four relatively distinct islands of research appear, at first blush, to be at different stages in their development. Scholars working in intergovernmental relations and co-production focus largely on describing and comparing the institutional arrangements intended to facilitate cooperation. Shared service research tends to ask whether service sharing in its various guises delivers a saving in cost. The wicked issues programme of work, by contrast, seems the most advanced in trying to understand the contingencies – whether at the environment, institutional or behavioural level – associated with improved performance.

Public management does not, however, enjoy exclusivity in its study of networks and partnership. Collaborative governance is also researched from other disciplinary perspectives which, in place of the performance agenda so in vogue with public administration scholars, focus more on questions of politics and power. Writing within this tradition, Davies and Spicer (2015, p. 235) refuse, as they put it, to join the 'celebrations of network governance' and suggest instead that the partnership agenda has been mis-sold to lower tiers of government and their communities. Behind the talk of trust and empowerment, Davies and Spicer (2015, p. 234) suggest that 'the ideology of networks' might be 'a rhetorical sleight of hand that obscures historic continuities in power relations and governing strategies'. Under the cover of the network 'metaphor' (Grote 2012), governments have continued to script the activities of local agencies in hierarchical ways and they have used these hierarchical instruments, in particular, to advance processes of privatisation and neo-liberal responsibilisation.

While the tendency to rebrand or relabel contracting-type arrangements as partnerships chimes with Davies and Spicer's critique (Hodge & Greve 2010), even they recognise it would be wrong to dismiss the partnership agenda simply as a Trojan horse for the continued privatisation of the state. Partnership in its various guises does offer an alternative mode of governance. Public–private infrastructure partnerships aside, network forms of organisation cannot be adequately understood through the lens of bureaucratic, market or autonomous coordination. Davies and Spicer (2015) are surely right though to suggest that rather than investing singularly in markets, hierarchies or networks, researchers need to understand the way in which these modes are combined for different effects.

References

Agranoff, R. (2004). 'Autonomy, devolution and intergovernmental relations'. *Regional & Federal Studies*, 14(1), 26–65.

Agranoff, R. (2007). *Managing Within Networks: Adding Value to Public Organizations*. Washington, DC: Georgetown University Press.

Aldag, A. M., Warner, M. E., & Bel, G. (2020). 'It depends on what you share: The elusive cost savings from service sharing'. *Journal of Public Administration Research and Theory*, 30(2), 275–289.

Alford, J., & Yates, S. (2016). 'Co-production of public services in Australia: The roles of government organisations and co-producers'. *Australian Journal of Public Administration*, 75(2), 159–175.

Allen, B., Tamindael, L. E., Bickerton, S. H., & Cho, W. (2020). 'Does citizen coproduction lead to better urban services in smart cities projects? An empirical study on e-participation in a mobile big data platform'. *Government Information Quarterly*, 37(1), 1–10.

Andrews, R., & Entwistle, T. (2010). 'Does cross-sectoral partnership deliver? An empirical exploration of public service effectiveness, efficiency, and equity'. *Journal of Public Administration Research and Theory*, 20(3), 679–701.

Bauer, A., & Steurer, R. (2014). 'Multi-level governance of climate change adaptation through regional partnerships in Canada and England'. *Geoforum*, 51, 121–129.

Bel, G., & Warner, M. E. (2015). 'Inter-municipal cooperation and costs: Expectations and evidence'. *Public Administration*, 93(1), 52–67.

Bel, G., & Sebő, M. (2021). 'Does inter-municipal cooperation really reduce delivery costs? An empirical evaluation of the role of scale economies, transaction costs, and governance arrangements'. *Urban Affairs Review*, 57(1), 153–188.

Benz, A., & Sonnicksen, J. (2018) 'Advancing backwards: Why institutional reform of German federalism reinforced joint decision-making'. *Publius: The Journal of Federalism*, 48(1), 134–159.

Boon, J. (2018). 'Moving the governance of shared service centres (SSCs) forward: Juxtaposing agency theory and stewardship theory'. *Public Money & Management*, 38(2), 97–104.

Börzel, T. A. (2000). 'From competitive regionalism to cooperative federalism: The Europeanization of the Spanish state of the autonomies'. *Publius: The Journal of Federalism*, 30(2), 17–42.

Bovaird, T., & Loeffler, E. (2012). 'From engagement to co-production: The contribution of users and communities to outcomes and public value'. *Voluntas: International Journal of Voluntary and Nonprofit Organizations*, 23(4), 1119–1138.

Brudney, J., & England, R. (1983). 'Toward a definition of the co-production concept'. *Public Administration Review*, 43(1), 59–65.

Bulpitt, J. (1986). 'The discipline of the new democracy: Mrs Thatcher's domestic statecraft'. *Political Studies*, 34(1), 19–39.

Cherney, A. (2004). 'Crime prevention/community safety partnerships in action: Victorian experience'. *Current Issues in Criminal Justice*, 15(3), 237–252.

Choi, I., & Moynihan, D. (2019). 'How to foster collaborative performance management? Key factors in the US federal agencies'. *Public Management Review*, 21(10), 1538–1559.

Corwin, E. (1933). 'Congress's power to prohibit commerce: A crucial constitutional issue'. *Cornell Law Quarterly*, 18(4), 477–506.

Cristofoli, D., Meneguzzo, M., & Riccucci, N. (2017). 'Collaborative administration: The management of successful networks'. *Public Management Review*, 19(3), 275–283.

Davies, J. S., & Spicer, A. (2015). 'Interrogating networks: Towards an agnostic perspective on governance research'. *Environment and Planning C: Government and Policy*, 33(2), 223–238.

Davis, J. H., Schoorman, F. D., & Donaldson, L. (1997). 'Toward a stewardship theory of Management'. *Academy of Management Review*, 22(1), 20–47.

de Sousa Santos, B. (1998). 'Participatory budgeting in Porto Alegre: Toward a redistributive democracy'. *Politics & Society*, 26(4), 461–510.

Dixon, R., & Elston, T. (2020). 'Efficiency and legitimacy in collaborative public management: Mapping inter-local agreements in England using social network analysis'. *Public Administration*, 98(3), 746–767.

Dollery, B., & Fleming, E. (2006). 'A conceptual note on scale economies, size economies and scope economies in Australian local government'. *Urban Policy and Research*, 24(2), 271–282.

Dollery, B., Grant, B., & Crase, L. (2011). 'Love thy neighbour: a social capital approach to local government partnerships', *Australian Journal of Public Administration*, 70(2), 156–166.

Dore, R. (1983). 'Goodwill and the spirit of market capitalism'. *The British Journal of Sociology*, 34(4), 459–482.

Elazar, D. J. (1964). 'Federal-state collaboration in the nineteenth-century United States'. *Political Science Quarterly*, 79(2), 248–281.

Elston, T., & Dixon, R. (2020). 'The effect of shared service centers on administrative intensity in English local government: A longitudinal evaluation'. *Journal of Public Administration Research and Theory*, 30(1), 113–129.

Entwistle, T., Bristow, G., Hines, F., Donaldson, S., & Martin, S. (2007). 'The dysfunctions of markets, hierarchies and networks in the meta-governance of partnership'. *Urban Studies*, 44(1), 63–79.

Entwistle, T., Downe, J., Guarneros-Meza, V., & Martin, S. (2014). 'The multi-level governance of Wales: Layer cake or marble cake?'. *The British Journal of Politics and International Relations*, 16(2), 310–325.

Fawcett, P., & Marsh, D. (2017). 'Rethinking federalism: Network governance, multi-level governance and Australian politics'. In Daniell, K. A. & Kay, A. (Eds.), *Multi-Level Governance*, Canberra: Australian National University Press, 57–79.

Ferlie, E., Fitzgerald, L., McGivern, G., Dopson, S., & Bennett, C. (2011). 'Public policy networks and "wicked problems": A nascent solution?'. *Public Administration*, 89(2), 307–324.

Gaudreault-DesBiens, J., & Poirier, J. (2017). 'From dualism to cooperative federalism and back?'. In Oliver, P., Macklem, P., & Des Rosiers, N. (Eds.), *The Oxford Handbook of the Canadian Constitution*, Oxford: Oxford University Press, 391–414.

Gaventa, J., & Barrett, G. (2012). 'Mapping the outcomes of citizen engagement'. *World Development*, 40(12), 2399–2410.

Grote, J. R. (2012). 'Horizontalism, vertical integration and vertices in governance networks'. *Stato e Mercato*, 32(1), 103–134.

Harguindéguy, J. B., Rivera, C. F., & Sánchez, A. S. (2021). 'So close yet so far: Intergovernmental tensions in Spain'. *Regional Studies*, 55(5), 894–906.

Hefetz, A., & Warner, M. E. (2012). 'Contracting or public delivery? The importance of service, market, and management characteristics'. *Journal of Public Administration Research and Theory*, 22(2), 289–231.

Hjern, B., & Porter, D. O. (1981). 'Implementation structures: A new unit of administrative analysis'. *Organization Studies*, 2(3), 211–227.

Hodge, G., & Greve, C. (2010). 'Public-private partnerships: Governance scheme or language game?'. *Australian Journal of Public Administration*, 69, S8–S22.

Hood, C. (2000). *The Art of the State: Culture, Rhetoric, and Public Management*. Oxford: Oxford University Press.

Hooghe, L., & Marks, G. (2003). 'Unravelling the central state, but how? Types of multi-level governance'. *American Political Science Review*, 97(2), 233–243.

James, O., & Jilke, S. (2020). 'Marketization reforms and co-production: Does ownership of service delivery structures and customer language matter?'. *Public Administration*, 98(4), 941–957.

Jaspers, S., & Steen, T. (2019). 'Realizing public values: Enhancement or obstruction? Exploring value tensions and coping strategies in the co-production of social care'. *Public Management Review*, 21(4), 606–627.

Kalesnikaite, V., & Neshkova, M. I. (2021). 'Problem severity, collaborative stage, and partner selection in US Cities'. *Journal of Public Administration Research and Theory*, 31(2), 399–415.

Keast, R., Brown, K., & Mandell, M. (2007). 'Getting the right mix: Unpacking integration meanings and strategies'. *International Public Management Journal*, 10(1), 9–33.

Kincaid, J. (1990). 'From cooperative to coercive federalism'. *The Annals of the American Academy of Political and Social Science*, 509(1), 139–152.

Klijn, E-H., Steijn, B., & Edelenbos, J. (2010). 'The impact of network management on outcomes in governance networks'. *Public Administration*, 88(4), 1063–1082.

Kropp, S., & Behnke, N. (2016). 'Marble cake dreaming of layer cake: The merits and pitfalls of disentanglement in German federalism reform'. *Regional & Federal Studies*, 26(5), 667–686.

Lindgreen, A., Koenig-Lewis, N., Kitchener, M., Brewer, J. D., Moore, M. H., & Meynhardt, T. (Eds.). (2019). *Public Value: Deepening, Enriching, and Broadening the Theory and Practice*. London: Routledge.

Ling, T. (2002). 'Delivering joined-up government in the UK: Dimensions, issues and problems'. *Public Administration*, 80(4), 615–642.

Macadam, E. (1934). 'The relations between the statutory and voluntary social services'. *Public Administration*, 12(3), 305–313.

Molina, O., & Rhodes, M. (2002). 'Corporatism: The past, present, and future of a concept'. *Annual Review of Political Science*, 5(1), 305–331.

Moore, M. H. (1995). *Creating Public Value: Strategic Management in Government*. Cambridge, MA: Harvard University Press.

McEwen, N. (2017). 'Still better together? Purpose and power in intergovernmental councils in the UK'. *Regional & Federal Studies*, 27(5), 667–690.

McEwen, N., Kenny, M., Sheldon, J., & Brown Swan, C. (2020). 'Intergovernmental relations in the UK: time for a radical overhaul?'. *The Political Quarterly*, 91(3), 632–640.

McGuire, M. (2002). 'Managing networks: Propositions on what managers do and why they do it'. *Public Administration Review*, 62(5), 599–609.

Nabatchi, T., Sancino, A., & Sicilia, M. (2017). 'Varieties of participation in public services: The who, when, and what of coproduction'. *Public Administration Review*, 77(5), 766–776.

Neshkova, M. I., & Guo, H. (2012). 'Public participation and organizational performance: Evidence from state agencies'. *Journal of Public Administration Research and Theory*, 22(2), 267–288.

Noland, J., & Phillips, R. (2010). 'Stakeholder engagement, discourse ethics and strategic management'. *International Journal of Management Reviews*, 12(1), 39–49.

Osborne, S. P. (2006). 'The new public governance?'. *Public Management Review*, 8(3), 377–387.

Osborne, S. P., Radnor, Z., & Nasi, G. (2013). 'A new theory for public service management? Toward a (public) service-dominant approach'. *The American Review of Public Administration*, 43(2), 135–158.

Pérez-López, G., Prior, D., Zafra-Gómez, J. L., & Plata-Díaz, A. M. (2016). 'Cost efficiency in municipal solid waste service delivery. Alternative management forms in relation to local population size'. *European Journal of Operational Research*, 255(2), 583–592.

Peters, B. G. (2017). 'What is so wicked about wicked problems? A conceptual analysis and a research program'. *Policy and Society*, 36(3), 385–396.

Phillimore, J., & Fenna, A. (2017). 'Intergovernmental councils and centralization in Australian federalism'. *Regional & Federal Studies*, 27(5), 597–621.

Provan, K. G., & Lemaire, R. H. (2012). 'Core concepts and key ideas for understanding public sector organizational networks: Using research to inform scholarship and practice'. *Public Administration Review*, 72(5), 638–648.

Provan, K. G., & Milward, H. B. (1995). 'A preliminary theory of network effectiveness: A comparative study of four community mental health systems'. *Administrative Science Quarterly*, 40(1), 1-23.

Rittel, H. W., & Webber, M. M. (1973). 'Dilemmas in a general theory of planning'. *Policy Sciences*, 4(2), 155–169.

Scharpf, F. W. (1988). 'The joint-decision trap: Lessons from German federalism and European integration'. *Public Administration*, 66(3), 239–278.

Selden, S. C., Sowa, J. E., & Sandfort, J. (2006). 'The impact of nonprofit collaboration in early child care and education on management and program outcomes'. *Public Administration Review*, 66(3), 412–425.

Sheldon, S. B., & Epstein, J. L. (2005). 'Involvement counts: Family and community partnerships and mathematics achievement'. *The Journal of Educational Research*, 98(4), 196–207.

Siciliano, M. D., Carr, J. B., & Hugg, V. G. (2021). 'Analyzing the effectiveness of networks for addressing public problems: Evidence from a longitudinal study'. *Public Administration Review*, forthcoming.

Spoor, A. (1939). 'The public's part in administration'. *Public Administration*, 17(2), 149–163.

Steen, T., Brandsen, T., & Verschuere, B. (2018). 'The dark side of co-creation and co-production: seven evils'. In Brandsen, T., Steen, T., & Verschuere, B. (Eds.), *Co-Production and Co-Creation. Engaging Citizens in Public Services*, London: Routledge, 284–293.

Stoker, G. (2006). 'Public value management: A new narrative for networked governance?'. *American Review of Public Administration*, 36(1), 41–57.

Stone, C. N. (1993). 'Urban regimes and the capacity to govern: A political economy approach'. *Journal of Urban Affairs*, 15(1), 1–28.

Swenden, W., & McEwen, N. (2014). 'UK devolution in the shadow of hierarchy? Intergovernmental relations and party politics'. *Comparative European Politics*, 12(4–5), 488–509.

Thomas, J. C. (2013). 'Citizen, customer, partner: Rethinking the place of the public in public management'. *Public Administration Review*, 73(6), 786–796.

Tomkinson, R. (2007). *Shared Services in Local Government.* Aldershot: Gower.

Turrini, A., Cristofoli, D., Frosini, F., & Nasi, G. (2010). 'Networking literature about determinants of network effectiveness'. *Public Administration,* 88(2), 528–550.

Vangen, S., & Huxham, C. (2003). 'Enacting leadership for collaborative advantage: Dilemmas of ideology and pragmatism in the activities of partnership managers'. *British Journal of Management,* 14(s), 61–76.

Voorberg, W., Jilke, S., Tummers, L., & Bekkers, V. (2018). 'Financial rewards do not stimulate coproduction: Evidence from two experiments'. *Public Administration Review,* 78(6), 864–873.

Warner, M. E., Aldag, A. M., & Kim, Y. (2020). 'Privatization and intermunicipal cooperation in US local government services: Balancing fiscal stress, need and political interests'. *Public Management Review,* forthcoming. https://doi.org/10.1080/14719037.2020.1751255

Watts, R. L. (2006). 'Origins of cooperative and competitive federalism'. In Greer, S. (Ed.), *Territory Democracy and Justice,* London: Palgrave Macmillan, 201–223.

Wildavsky, A. (1973). 'If planning is everything, maybe it's nothing'. *Policy Sciences,* 4(2), 127–153.

Wood, S. (2000). 'Why indicative planning failed'. *Twentieth Century British History,* 11(4), 431–459.

6 Changing agendas of public management research

This book has argued that public management research continues to plough furrows first established by the founding fathers of the discipline. All four of the themes considered in the book – bureaucracy, markets, autonomy and collaboration – were familiar to classical management theorists. That the central planks of public administration have remained in place despite the huge change in the focus and scale of government through the twentieth century is in many ways remarkable. There have of course been important changes in our use and understanding of each of the four forms of organisation through that time.

As predicted by Weber, the twentieth century saw a rapid expansion in the scale and scope of bureaucratic administration. While the new public management prompted the privatisation, outsourcing and unbundling of many state-owned bureaucratic services, the private organisations which have taken their place continue to rely on bureaucratic methods for large-scale service delivery. The enthusiasm for new organisational forms has in this sense been sedimented onto persisting forms of bureaucratic administration. Researchers meanwhile have, following Merton (1936) and Simon's (1944) lead, continued to unpick the bureaucratic principles laid down by Weber by studying the dysfunctional consequences of formalisation, accountability and merit. Performance management and PSM have been treated more positively but even here researchers increasingly focus on bureaucracy's dysfunctional or dark side. While this research effort has given us a hugely more sophisticated appreciation of the ways in which bureaucracy goes wrong, only tangentially does it explain bureaucracy's persistence and success. Some theorists have started to rally to bureaucracy's defence, but empirical investigations of the continuing functional success of bureaucracy are still thin on the ground.

In part reflecting an increasing awareness of the problems of bureaucracy, governments have since the late twentieth century privatised and outsourced large parts of what used to be the state. Although the cost and quality effects of privatisation have been extensively researched, we know much less of how this change of ownership has affected the processes of administration. Do ideas like representative bureaucracy, accountability and public service motivation transfer to the private sector bureaucracies increasingly tasked with public service delivery? Hodson et al. (2013) study of private sector bureaucracies gives some reasons to think that privately owned bureaucracy might be more Kafkaesque than Weberian. Alongside and sometimes in place of privatisation and outsourcing, governments have also shown remarkable ingenuity in the creation of market-like conditions. Operating in quasi-market-type environments, formally public organisations have adopted the cultural attributes – in terms of entrepreneurialism and the prioritisation of organisational survival – of private sector organisations. The intermingling or bending (Dees & Anderson 2003) of public and private sectors and bureaucratic and entrepreneurial forms of management warns against simplistic binary accounts of marketisation. Some privatised services maintain many of the hallmarks of publicness while some state-owned services operate in a highly marketised manner (Bozeman & Bretschneider 1994). While the blurring of the boundary between public and private sectors is extraordinary, the problems of the market – from imperfect competition to moral hazard – are very familiar.

Autonomy has just as ancient a lineage as bureaucracy and markets but only recently has it started to receive the research attention it deserves. Catapulted into the spotlight by the new public management's fashion for the unbundling of government into separate agencies, ideas of organisational or managerial autonomy now provide the guiding thread for the reform of service delivery organisations from schools to leisure centres. As new kids on the block, autonomy researchers have made huge progress in a short space of time. Much of the work has been invested into classificatory questions of how autonomy can be defined and measured and subsequently whether or not it delivers any of advantages reformers promise. Not enough work yet accepts autonomy for the established management technique that it is and tries to understand the way that it works in different contexts. There will no doubt be circumstances conducive to autonomy-type reforms and circumstances which are less fortuitous, at the minute though we are only just beginning to understand these contingencies.

Again, bracketing off a largely informal prehistory, the formal adoption of collaborative governance has enjoyed a prominent position in public management for some time. The cooperative approach to intergovernmental relations and peak-level negotiation is particularly well established. More recently, however, governments have formally adopted the partnership model as a way of delivering mainstream policy. Perhaps reflecting a slightly longer history, research into networks has – with the possible exception of that on co-production – largely moved beyond questions of classification and simple functionality. Increasingly, network and partnership research points to the contingent relationship between aspects of structure and context.

Other changes have of course occurred alongside the evolution of these forms of organisation. This chapter looks at changes in the context of public management, the emergence of new instruments and changes in form and approach to research. This chapter concludes with a brief discussion of the future of the discipline.

Changing contexts

Anyone living through the COVID-19 pandemic of 2020–2021 is painfully aware of how rapidly and dramatically our times can change. Almost all states have put in place extraordinarily draconian curfew legislation to close down social activity and keep people in their homes in a bid to contain the spread of COVID-19. Governments have at the same time committed to unprecedented levels of borrowing to support whole industries and huge swathes of the working population with transfer payments of one form or another. Public managers have largely done these things with the same old instruments of bureaucracy (in terms of policing behaviour, distributing PPE, tests and vaccines), markets (for the procurement of PPE, test and trace, new health infrastructure) and collaboration (between governments, researchers and the pharmaceutical industry). COVID-19, in a way only seen in the world wars of the twentieth century, has registered a new high-water mark in the power and extent of the state.

As if that was not enough the UK has juggled the COVID-19 pandemic with the huge constitutional change of departing from the European Union. The consequences in terms of trade and the movement of people are already becoming apparent. But shedding the uppermost tier of its system of multi-level governance has profound significance too for policy areas (like agriculture and the environment) which for nearly fifty years have been framed in a European context. It is not at all clear how much policy autonomy the UK government has won through Brexit or to what extent it plans to use it. It is clear, however, that departure from the EU has profound implications for the relationships between the levels of government that remain. Relations between London and the devolved governments of Scotland, Wales and Northern Ireland have all been worsened by Brexit (McEwen et al. 2020). A situation made more alarming still by the fragile institutions of intergovernmental relations through which new relationships will need to be negotiated.

All of these things have happened against a backdrop of the increasingly fast-moving environmental disaster of global warming and an ongoing mass extinction event (Ceballos et al. 2020). Governments have responded to the threat of global warming in collaborative ways. Signatories to the Paris agreement effectively volunteered to develop their own emission control strategies which in theory at least would collectively limit further global warming to 2°C (Morgan 2016). Progress in the achievement of that goal depends entirely on the national strategies developed by each signatory. These strategies in turn depend upon the age old mechanisms provided by hierarchies, markets and networks reviewed in this book. Hierarchical instruments are used to prescribe (or proscribe) carbon friendly (or unfriendly) technologies. Arrangements to facilitate the trade in carbon emissions have been instituted on the presumption that a market for Carbon will drive reductions in emissions as if by an invisible hand. We have all been persuaded to voluntarily adopt more sustainable practices from walking more to eating less meat. It is not an exaggeration to say that our futures depend upon the effectiveness of these instruments. We already know, however, that the agreements and the instruments underwriting the Paris agreement are subject to all of the dysfunctions touched on in this book.

The effectiveness of government responses to COVID-19, global warming and Brexit depend greatly upon the relationship between governments and their citizens but that too is undergoing substantial change. Researchers in the US (Iyengar 2019) and Europe (Reiljan 2020, p. 376) point to 'an increased partisan animosity' between supporters of opposing political parties which Iyengar (2019) dubs 'affective polarisation'. Whether driven by the extreme stances of political leaders or the divisive effects of social media, an increasing body of evidence points to a 'partisan animus' which 'might spill over and affect behaviors and attitudes outside the political realm' (Iyengar et al. 2019, p. 136). Affective polarisation might be eroding the capacity of the state to recruit its citizens as co-producers. Bearing this out, Grossman et al. (2020) find that compliance with physical distancing recommendations of state governors varied with citizen partisanship.

The problem of affective polarisation is intimately entwined with a turn to populism observed across a number of democracies. Although definitions are contested, Mudde and Rovira Kaltwasser (2018, p. 1669) suggest an ideational approach which treats populism as a thin ideology that 'not only depicts society as divided between "the pure people" versus "the corrupt elite", but also claims that politics is about respecting popular sovereignty at any cost'. Because populists, as Mudde and Rovira Kaltwasser (2018) explain, 'have serious problems with liberal democracy, most notably minority rights, rule of law, and separation of powers (including independence of the judiciary and the media)', populism also sits uncomfortably with the central planks of public management. Populism, particularly when aligned with affective polarisation, might not only make it difficult to deliver behaviour change, but it may also spill over into a greater antagonism to public managers and the institutions they work in.

Tackling issues like global warming with a more polarised citizenry which is more suspicious of state institutions sounds like a recipe for a challenging century for public managers. There are, however, some glimmers of light on the horizon.

Changing instruments

The public managers of the twenty-first century may, however, be helped by the emergence of new instruments. A fast-paced revolution in ICT embracing 'mobile applications, open data, social media, technical and organizational networks, the Internet of things, sensors, data analytics' is continually providing government with novel ways of administering public policy (Gil-Garcia et al. 2018, p. 634). In the case of COVID-19 it is increasingly clear, after some false starts, that mobile phone applications offer an alternative to manual approaches to the control of disease transmission (Nurtay et al. 2020). Dunleavy et al. (2006) argue that digital era governance has replaced the fragmenting tendencies of the new public management with an emphasis on digital reintegration in which radically re-engineered processes provide, as Gil-Garcia et al. (2018, p. 633) put it, 'more efficient, transparent, and effective government'. Gil Garcia et al. (2018, p. 633) argue that the extent of digitalisation is such that: 'It is hard to imagine any government function or governance process that does not involve extensive use of information and technology'. As Gil-Garcia et al. (2018) suggest developments in ICT have not only transformed service delivery. Their review of the literature also points to significant changes in management, policy and democracy. The latter of these seems particularly significant in the extent to which it affords greater opportunities for citizen engagement and co-production.

Developments in ICT do not, however, inevitably make every-thing easier or better. Often times they merely re-present existing systems, choices and problems. In such a way, Dahlberg (2011) identifies four different types or varieties of digital democracy from the liberal-individualist to autonomist Marxist. He finds, however, to date a 'near-universal hegemony of the liberal-individualist interpretation of the democratic subject and democracy' (Dahlberg 2011, p. 866). Otherwise expressed, it is the liberal-individualist form of democracy with its mechanisms of 'aggregating, calculating, choosing, competing, expressing, fundraising, informing, petitioning, registering, transacting, transmitting, voting' which has triumphed in the move online over more deliberative and cooperative forms of democracy (Dahlberg 2011, p. 865). Andrews (2019) goes so far as to suggest that the algorithms at the heart of digital services (whether they be public or private) raise a series of risks which amount to a new 'wicked problem'.

Not all the new instruments of public policy are electronic. Thaler and Sunstein have argued that behaviour change can be delivered through relatively subtle (and crucially low cost) changes in 'choice architecture' (Thaler & Sunstein 2008). Nudges built into the way in which information is presented to decision-makers can prompt people to make better decisions both for themselves and for society at large. Nudges are much cheaper than traditional policy interventions which rely on the employment of bureaucrats and professionals to deliver policy outputs of one form or another, but they also have the considerable virtue that they engage directly with the human behaviour which generates the social problem and in turn its potential solution (John 2018). Nudges have been tested in a bewildering range of contexts oftentimes with positive results but critics question first whether positive results in nudge experiments can be translated into the field; whether they can do anything about the big problems of poverty, crime, education and ill health which soak up the lion-share of public spending; and, finally, whether subliminal influences on behaviour are ethical (Hausman & Welch 2010; Entwistle 2021).

By putting behaviour at the heart of policy design, nudge provides an important corrective to the grand policy designs of the twentieth century. In place of elaborate interventions premised on the smooth working of bureaucracies and markets, nudge promises to deconstruct policies into a series of micro-interventions. In such a way, it affords a bespoke approach to policy-making in which mixes of different instruments are matched to the circumstances of specific target communities. In many ways this acknowledges the existing reality of most policy interventions. Without any coherent philosophy, the suite of policies associated with the new public management bequeathed hybrid policy designs which variously appealed to notions of autonomy, competition and regulation. It is the mix of these different elements which made the new public management policies so difficult to evaluate. The behavioural approach to research underlying nudge provides the opportunity to unpack these different effects and to understand the way in which they may interact. While a number of scholars have called for a recognition of the way in which the idealised approaches of hierarchies, markets and networks are mixed into hybrid arrangements of one form or another (Keast et al. 2006; Davies & Spicer 2015), at this stage we know little about the way this works in practice. Hybrid arrangements have been treated more as a research problem than as an opportunity.

Changing research

Alongside changes in the context and instruments of public policy, public management's research methods are changing too. The early years of the discipline – as indicated by the back issues of the leading, and now venerable journals in the field – were characterised by a close engagement with practitioners and a tendency to describe administrative arrangements that prevailed in different countries. Over time, however, public administration research has become both more theoretical, more empirically sophisticated and more comparative in its orientation. Unfortunately, however, developments in these three regards have not served to deepen the relationship between research and practice. Quite the reverse in fact, public management research is now criticised for its increasing detachment from practice (Carboni et al. 2019). The discipline continues to change, however, and some of the new avenues might bring research and practice closer together. Four developments seem particularly important.

The enthusiasm for nudge reported in the preceding section is significant for at least two reasons. First, it promises to bring scholars and practitioners back together. Nudge appeals to practitioners because it offers cheap, easy and effective ways of delivering behaviour change. Second, it appeals to researchers because of the behavioural research methods that lie behind it. The new sub-field of behavioural public administration seeks to build our knowledge of behaviour change through sometimes really quite simple experiments and pilots (James et al. 2017; James et al. 2020). In place of the challenge of isolating the separate effects of different instruments and contexts found in real-world policy settings, behavioural public administration promises the superior methods of experiments and randomised controlled trials.

Public administration does not, however, enjoy a monopoly in the field, as ever public administration has adopted much of the science behind nudge from scholars working in economics and psychology.

The second key development in methods stems from the huge growth in the availability of organisational information of various forms. Historically public management research was hampered by the absence of performance information that was readily available for private sector management researchers. Beyond simple description, public management researchers relied on surveys to provide data for both their independent and dependent variables. Government enthusiasm for measuring and classifying performance means increasingly that it is possible to use independently (and often audited) measures of performance free from the disadvantages of common source bias. Qualitative researchers too can readily access a wealth of data from inspection reports to public inquiries which allow extraordinary depth without the need for time-consuming and often flawed methods of data collection. Hopkins (2006) makes the case that the wealth of data collected in inquiries and archived on the web might even allow a kind of virtual ethnography without all of the profound problems of its real-world namesake.

Third, comparative research goes from strength to strength. But rather than using the comparative method to generate insights into the idiosyncrasies of particular national traditions of public administration, researchers increasingly find they can study the same or very similar phenomena in different national contexts. The homogenising effects of the new public management and subsequent fashions means that almost all countries pursue a similar and comparable suite of public management reforms. This globalisation of the instruments of public management is such that the co-production of sustainable waste management practices in China (Lu & Sidortsov 2019) is readily comparable to similar practices in Brazil (Gutberlet 2015). Global data sets even allow for comparisons to be made against common yardsticks. This does not mean that reforms work in the same way in different settings, but it does provide us with a way of understanding the way in which different contexts serve to influence outcomes (Meier et al. 2017).

The survey of work contained in this book points to a fourth conclusion related to the paradoxical nature of the public management discipline. Simply expressed although much public management work asks functional questions about the way in which public services are managed (whether through bureaucracy, collaboration and so on), it oftentimes finds dysfunctional effects. Even though we as scholars know that many of the ideas we study persist for reasons other than effectiveness, we continue to give them the benefit of the doubt and study them on the presumption of their functionality. While there is some benefit in repeatedly underlining the finding that processes of marketisation have dysfunctional effects or the sharing of back office functions does not actually save costs, we also need work which explains why these ideas are as successful and persistent as they are. If marketisation is not really about improving efficiency, why do governments repeatedly resort to market forms of organisation?

In asking this more critical question, public management as a discipline needs to maintain its focus not just on the management of public services but also the broader management of people both as service producers and consumers (Moynihan 2018). In this manner, it is possible, for example, that marketisation provides a good way of managing the state even if it does not offer the most efficient way of delivering public services. The Foucauldian idea of governmentality focuses on this question by considering the way in which 'individuals' beliefs, desires, lifestyles and actions' are 'shaped, directed and regulated' by diverse 'technologies of power' (Bevir 2011, p. 461). Although the idea of governmentality has been taken up at the fringes of the public management discipline (Miller & Rose 2008; Ferlie & McGivern 2014), there are reasons to think that the challenges of the twenty-first century – from global pandemics to global warming – need us to put the question of how we make people and problems governable centre stage.

References

Andrews, L. (2019). 'Public Administration, public leadership and the construction of public value in the age of the algorithm and "big data"'. *Public Administration*, 97(2), 296–310.

Bevir, M. (2011). 'Governance and governmentality after neoliberalism'. *Policy & Politics*. 39(4), 457–471.

Bozeman, B., & Bretschneider, S. (1994). 'The "publicness puzzle" in organization theory: A test of alternative explanations of differences between public and private organizations'. *Journal of Public Administration Research and Theory*, 4(2), 197–224.

Carboni, J. L., Dickey, T., Moulton, S., O'keefe, S., O'leary, R., Piotrowski, S. J., & Sandfort, J. (2019). 'Start with the problem: Establishing research relevance with integrative public administration'. *Perspectives on Public Management and Governance*, 2(4), 267–274.

Ceballos, G., Ehrlich, P. R., & Raven, P. H. (2020). 'Vertebrates on the brink as indicators of biological annihilation and the sixth mass extinction'. *Proceedings of the National Academy of Sciences*, 117(24), 13596–13602.

Dahlberg, L. (2011). 'Re-constructing digital democracy: An outline of four "positions"'. *New Media & Society*, 13(6), 855–872.

Davies, J. S., & Spicer, A. (2015). 'Interrogating networks: Towards an agnostic perspective on governance research'. *Environment and Planning C: Government and Policy*, 33(2), 223–238.

Dees, J. G., & Anderson, B. B. (2003). 'Sector bending: Blurring lines between non-profit and for-profit'. *Society*, 40(4), 16-27.

Dunleavy, P., Margetts, H., Bastow, S., & Tinkler, J. (2006). 'New public management is dead – long live digital-era governance'. *Journal of Public Administration Research and Theory*, 16(3), 467–494.

Entwistle, T. (2021). 'Why nudge sometimes fails: Fatalism and the problem of behaviour change'. *Policy and Politics*, 49(1), 87–103.

Ferlie, E., & McGivern, G. (2014). 'Bringing Anglo-governmentality into public management scholarship: The case of evidence-based medicine in UK health care'. *Journal of Public Administration Research and Theory*, 24(1), 59–83.

Ferretti, L., Wynant, C., Kendall, M., Zhao, L., Nurtay, A., Abeler-Dörner, L., Parker, M., Bonsall, D., & Fraser, C. (2020). 'Quantifying SARS-CoV-2 transmission suggests epidemic control with digital contact tracing'. *Science*, 368(6491), 1–9.

Gil-Garcia, J.R., Dawes, S.S., & Pardo, T.A. (2018). 'Digital government and public management research: finding the crossroads'. *Public Management Review*, 20(5), 633–646.

Grossman, G., Kim, S., Rexer, J. M., & Thirumurthy, H. (2020). 'Political partisanship influences behavioral responses to governors' recommendations for COVID-19 prevention in the United States'. *Proceedings of the National Academy of Sciences*, 117(39), 24144–24153.

Gutberlet, J. (2015). 'More inclusive and cleaner cities with waste management co-production: Insights from participatory epistemologies and methods'. *Habitat International*, 46, 234–243.

Hausman, D. M., & Welch, B. (2010). 'Debate: To nudge or not to nudge'. *Journal of Political Philosophy*, 18(1), 123–136.

Hodson, R., Roscigno, V. J., Martin, A., & Lopez, S. H. (2013). 'The ascension of Kafkaesque bureaucracy in private sector organizations'. *Human Relations*, 66(9), 1249–1273.

Hopkins, A. (2006). 'Studying organisational cultures'. *Safety Science*, 44(10), 875–889.

Iyengar, S., Lelkes, Y., Levendusky, M., Malhotra, N., & Westwood, S. J. (2019). 'The origins and consequences of affective polarization in the United States'. *Annual Review of Political Science*, 22, 129–146.

James, O., Jilke, S. R., & Van Ryzin, G. G. (Eds.). (2017). *Experiments in Public Management Research: Challenges and Contributions*. Cambridge: Cambridge University Press.

James, O., Olsen, A. L., Moynihan, D. P., & Van Ryzin, G. G. (2020). *Behavioral Public Performance: How People Make Sense of Government Metrics*. Cambridge: Cambridge University Press.

John, P. (2018). *How Far to Nudge? Assessing Behavioural Public Policy.* Cheltenham: Edward Elgar Publishing.

Keast, R., Mandell, M., & Brown, K. (2006). 'Mixing state, market and network governance modes: The role of government in "crowded" policy domains'. *International Journal of Organization Theory and Behavior*, 9(1), 27–50.

Lu, H., & Sidortsov, R. (2019). 'Sorting out a problem: A co-production approach to household waste management in Shanghai, China'. *Waste Management*, 95, 271–277.

McEwen, N., Kenny, M., Sheldon, J., & Brown Swan, C. (2020). 'Intergovernmental relations in the UK: time for a radical overhaul?' *The Political Quarterly*, 91(3), 632–640.

Meier, K. J., Rutherford, A., & Avellaneda, C. N. (Eds.). (2017). *Comparative Public Management: Why National, Environmental, and Organizational Context Matters.* Washington, DC: Georgetown University Press.

Merton, R. K. (1936). 'The unanticipated consequences of purposive social action'. *American Sociological Review*, 1(6), 894–904.

Miller, P. & Rose, N. (2008). *Governing the Present: Administering Economic, Social and Personal Life.* Cambridge: Polity Press.

Mudde, C., & Rovira Kaltwasser, C. (2018). 'Studying populism in comparative perspective: Reflections on the contemporary and future research agenda'. *Comparative Political Studies*, 51(13), 1667–1693.

Morgan, J. (2016). 'Paris COP 21: Power that speaks the truth?'. *Globalizations*, 13(6), 943–951.

Moynihan, D. (2018). 'A great schism approaching? Towards a micro and macro public administration'. *Journal of Behavioral Public Administration*, 1(1), 1–8.

Reiljan, A. (2020). '"Fear and loathing across party lines" (also) in Europe: Affective polarisation in European party systems'. *European Journal of Political Research*, 59(2), 376–396.

Simon, H. (1944). 'Decision making and administrative organizations'. *Public Administration Review*, 4(1), 16–30.

Thaler, R. H., & Sunstein, C. R. (2008). *Nudge: Improving Decisions About Health, Wealth, and Happiness.* New Haven, CT: Yale University Press.

Index

social problems 78, 79, 98
Soviet Union 17, 18
Spain 77, 81–2
stakeholder red tape 12
stewardship governance 83
strategic autonomy 45
Sweden 57, 63

target setting 11, 17–19
taut planning 18
Taylor, Frederick 17
teachers 13–14
technical efficiency 55
technical expertise/technocracy 11, 20–1, 39
technology 5; digital era 97–8
transaction costs 56, 57, 74

UK: Brexit 95–6; devolved governments 78, 96; intergovernmental relations 78,

96; NHS 41, 42, 63, 65, 79; private finance initiative 59
United States: American Public Administration 15; charter schools 37, 41; New York State 82
unit costs 82
universities 54, 63, 64

voluntarism 80

Waldo, Clifford Dwight 1
waste management 60, 81, 83, 100
water privatisation 60
Weber, Max 4, 6, 10, 11, 12, 15, 16, 17, 20, 22, 23, 24, 25, 26, 27, 93
wicked issues 7, 74, 75, 78–81
Wilson, Woodrow 6, 10, 11, 12, 15, 16, 17, 20, 22, 23, 24, 25, 26, 27

yardstick competition 7, 54, 64–7